PROFIT, Not Loss

The Financial Guide
for Women Business Owners

CHRISTINA GAMACHE

A note about the stories in this book: Stories are an essential part of every culture throughout history. The author included as many stories as possible to illustrate her points. She based the stories on actual events she has witnessed, then named the case study characters after her good friends. Any resemblance to actual people or situations is purely coincidental.

Prominence Publishing can be reached at www.prominencepublishing.com.

The author can be reached as follows: https:// www.growthconsultingfirm.com

Profit, Not Loss/ Christina Gamache. -- 1st ed.

ISBN: 978-1-990830-31-0

Dedication

For my girls. I believe in you!
Thank you, Andrew. I love you!

Table of Contents

Preface

The finance industry needs to help small business owner women. The Small Business Administration (SBA) defines a small business as a company that generates less than $10 million in annual revenue. The industry is also struggling to help women. In 1792, 24 male stock brokers founded the New York Stock Exchange, long before women's suffrage when women won the right to vote through the 19th amendment in 1920. Much has changed since then, but there are still many hurdles that women must jump over to gain the same level of services in the finance industry. Small businesses and women are two major and essential groups in our society. According to the SBA, small businesses account for 62% of job creation.[1] But The Exit Planning Institute states that 80 percent of these small business owners will not sell their business when it comes time for the owner to retire.[2] Many owners will liquidate their business assets and stop working when they are either forced to retire or choose to leave.

Only 10 percent of owners will sell their business for a value and then use that reward to help them retire. Some small business owners had "emergency liquidation sales" during the pandemic because they were either financially, physically, or emotionally unable to continue operating their businesses. On top of all this, women are statistically likely to end up alone at the end of their lives, whether due to death or divorce,[3] and therefore become the head of the household, if they aren't already. These women will become the sole provider for their families.

---

[1] https://advocacy.sba.gov/wp-content/uploads/2021/12/Small-Business-FAQ-Revised-December-2021.pdf

[2] https://exit-planning-institute.org/state-of-owner-readiness

[3] https://www.ubs.com/global/en/media/display-page-ndp/en-20190306-financial-security.html

In 2020, I had what I call a "Jerry McGuire moment." Remember when Tom Cruise's character freaks out and quits his job? I left a lucrative career in the financial services industry to support the business owners in my community. I saw an unmet need for women owners especially to know the basics about money, interpret their finances, make strategic decisions, and control their destiny to help them take care of the things that matter most.

I aim to help as many owners scale their businesses wisely and then sell their businesses successfully. Our jobs, careers, and businesses are simply vehicles we use to care for those who matter most to us. Author Simon Sinek says to "start with the why" behind everything you do. I disagree! I say to "start with *who*." Who matters to you the most? This person or these people will be the driving reason behind everything you do in life. Your "who" could be your family, friends, employees, neighbors, or yourself. Who do you run your business for? Who gets you up and out of bed every morning? Who motivates you to be your best? Who do you want or need to care for? Who do you look up to?

Who did I write this book for? First and foremost, I wrote this book for my two daughters. When they were younger, my oldest would tell me she wanted to do what I did when she grew up. At the time, I was working as an employee for a wire house and felt trapped and unsatisfied. I tried to be happy that my daughters saw value in what I was doing then, but it wasn't the life I wanted for either of them.

After I launched my business in 2020, they both came to me and said, "Mommy, we want to be like you when we grow up – a business owner"! My heart glowed with love and joy. They got to work quickly, and soon "B's Biscuits and Bandanas" and "D's Art Attack" were born. While I know they will have many ups and downs, becoming a business owner will be more satisfying for them in whatever industry they choose, even if

2

they decide to have a full-time job plus a side hustle. I hope this book will smooth out the volatility for them one day as they look to these words as a guide.

This book is also for women business owners who don't necessarily know how to interpret their finances, but they know without a doubt that they need the numbers to support their dreams. You are too small to hire a full-time CFO but too big to go at this alone. According to the Census Bureau, less than two percent of women-owned businesses make over a million dollars in annual revenue.[4] This book is for those women who want to break through this unknown glass ceiling and get their business to the next level.

I know who you are because I am very similar to you in many ways. You have big dreams and a big heart. You want or need to care for many people, maybe your parents, kids, employees, partners, and friends. You are a fierce participant in your community because you want to pave the way to a brighter future for the next generation. You are probably in your 40s or 50s and approaching the peak of your life. But you are also extremely busy. When do you have time to breathe? Fortunately, you know you didn't become a successful entrepreneur by doing everything yourself; you know how to delegate. This book is definitely for you. Let me show you how to use your finances to make strategic decisions in forecasting, keeping your thumb on the pulse of your business, knowing when a vendor or employee isn't doing their job, getting the maximum return on your investment, and scaling like a boss. You are the visionary and the CEO. Let me be your right-hand CFO. Let's go!

---

[4] https://www.census.gov/programs-surveys/abs.html

Introduction

A large financial firm[5] surveyed a few years ago about the state of women as it relates to their finances. What they discovered was astounding to me. Millennials are the most educated and empowered generation to date, and they are deciding not to be active in their financial prowess. Why? Millennial women are more likely to give up their financial powers to their spouses than Generation Xers and Baby Boomers.

When I first meet many clients, they tell me a dark secret. They have been coasting financially for decades, putting their head in the sand like an ostrich and trying to ignore their money situation. It worsens when these clients admit they also do this with their business. They know they need to pay attention to the dollars, but these clients acknowledge they need help understanding where to begin and how it all comes together.

Business owners are a different kind of breed from ordinary long-term employees. You are a risk-taker, a dreamer, and a leader. Because you think differently, you need a different type of advisor who understands where you are coming from and where you are going. Your assets are mostly in your business, and your livelihood depends on how well your business is doing. Your ability to be present with your family or friends is contingent upon the state of your company.

I want you to be confident about your numbers in the business and your personal life. You don't need to be an expert, but I will get you to the point where finances are manageable. Owners often already know the state of their affairs, but they can't precisely pinpoint their pain or success. I'll

---

[5] https://www.ubs.com/us/en/wealth-management/specialized-advice/women-and-finances.html#ourlatestinsights

show you what to pay attention to — in plain English! You'll use your financial information to grow your business. Gone are the days when advisors will talk over your head and ignore you — or, even worse — get annoyed by your questions and comments. This is a safe space designed to meet you where you are.

**A word about GAAP: Generally Accepted Accounting Procedures exist because of companies like Enron (a company that committed economy-shattering fraud many years ago). Fraud is a nasty scheme and is unfortunately on the rise. You don't want to burn up in "cooking the books" because you want to look good for investors or banks. Always take the high road, even if it's tough. You might not like what you see when we open your financial records. Your books will tell you a lot about what your business is all about. It's like lifting the hood of a car to see what's making it move. I'll walk you through general themes and ideas you could implement to improve your finances if they need revising to your standards. However, these ideas are legal and meant to enhance your business.

At the end of this book, you'll have all the tools necessary to make empowered decisions in your business and personal life. Should you hire a new employee? Should you expand into a new location? Should you retire early? Should you buy a second or third property? Can you afford to send your kids to college? Are you saving enough? Are your employees taken care of? Is your family taken care of? I'll show you how specific financial strategies can save or make you money!

Here's what you'll learn in this book:

Section I — Set the financial foundation

Section II — Learn to scale your business

Section III — Selling your business

Section I:
Set the Financial Foundation

Chapter 1

Goals: Start with the End

What do you want to achieve during your lifetime?

Growing up, my South Korean mother would combine lunar new year traditions with Western calendar new year traditions. Instead of celebrating the lunar new year on the lunar calendar (sometimes in January or February), we would celebrate the new year on January first. We would watch the ball drop in Times Square on New Year's Eve and eat rice cakes on New Year's Day. We would write New Year's resolutions and receive money in little red envelopes. However, before we could get our money, we would have to present our written New Year's resolutions and bow to our parents. After that, my parents would bless and give us those precious little envelopes.

This practice carried on with me through my adult life. Even though I now give envelopes of money to the next generation, I still write out all my New Year's resolutions and goals. I will write my goals by December 1. If I'm writing my goals for the following year on New Year's Eve, I'm behind.

There's a power to writing down your goals. Seeing your aspirations in black and white somehow makes them real. We've all seen those motivational posters about writing down goals. I wholeheartedly believe many are true, despite how corny they seem. The power of writing down your goals in black and white helps you visualize them. When you imagine your future, you can begin to make strides in the right direction. Elite athletes, top CEOs, and other successful icons all make goal-setting a priority and practically a devout dedication.

I make my clients write down their goals as well. I encourage them to go on a long walk or open a nice bottle of wine by themselves or with their partner and write down their goals. If you are married, complete this exercise with your spouse or life partner. Do this with your business partner if you are in business with someone. It's an eye-opening exercise and the first step in proper financial planning. Not only do financial problems rank as one of the top reasons for divorce, but it's also a topic not easily discussed. Often, partners will have different answers when they do this exercise. The purpose of the exercise is not to see how close you can get to the same answer. This activity will be a conversation starter for future discussions and planning. It's also a way to discover why we invest, save, and have a business. What are you working toward? When should you stop? Why would you stop?

One client recently told me that she doesn't like to write down her goals because she will feel disappointed if she doesn't achieve them. I understand that! My number one fear growing up was the fear of failure. I felt like a total loser if I failed. I would research and write draft after draft until I got it right. What would people say about me if I failed? If I fail, that must mean I am worthless and should give up!

The older I get, the more I realize there's so much I don't know. This lack of knowledge means I must try again at something I'm not yet an expert in. Failure to achieve your goals does not mean you should stop. It simply means that you are working in the right direction. You won't get everything right at first, and that's OK! Give yourself permission to learn from your mistakes and try again. Write down those goals. If you don't get there by the time you said you would, revise that goal and try again. Life is fluid and active. Goals should be, too.

If your child tells you she wants to learn how to ride a bicycle, do you ask her to give up when she falls for the first time? What do you say after she falls the second time? If your business doesn't achieve the goals you set, that's OK. But if you don't have any goals to begin with, then what the heck are you working toward? Why wouldn't you get a J.O.B. or flush all that money down the toilet? I know the future is never predictable, no matter how hard we try to control it. I also know that despite our goal setting, the outcomes will always be wildly different. Life changes and many factors beyond our reach will affect our journeys toward our goals. Still, I urge you to practice goal-setting in your own life.

I've developed resources for you to follow throughout this book. *Profit, Not Loss* isn't a passive program for you to watch. I want you to actively participate.

Whenever you see the download icon, you know a specific resource is waiting for you online at https://www.growthconsultingfirm.com/resources.

You're not alone on this journey. I hope you find solace in knowing that many business owners have had the same anxieties, fears, hopes, and dreams before you. And I'll be holding your hand throughout this book and beyond. So, let's jump into it. Head to the website right now and download your GOALS worksheet. Come back and follow along.

This is the fun part, so go wild! Let's break your goals down into three major categories. Call them your "Now," "Lifetime," and "Legacy" goals.

NOW GOALS

The first category is your short-term goals that are 12 to 60 months (one to five years) from now. What type of goals are you working toward now or in the near future? Some examples could be:

- Buy a home or a vacation home

- Send a kid to college

- Hire a VP of Finance

- Travel abroad regularly

- Start a new product line

- Buy a car

- Hire an executive assistant

Next to your goals, write the amount of money you think you need to succeed. Be realistic and research a reasonable dollar amount to plan for. For now, don't worry about where the money is coming from. Think only about what it would take to get you to your goal.

Buy a home or vacation home	$1,100,000 + $60,000 for renovations
Send a kid to college	$45,000 for a four-year degree
Hire a VP of Finance	$200,000 a year + benefits
Travel abroad regularly	$35,000 per overseas trip
Start a new product line	$60,000 initial investment
Buy a car	$50,000
Hire an executive assistant	$90,000 a year + benefits

LIFETIME GOALS

Lifetime goals are tricky because they can span several decades. Think about your dreams from the next five years until the end of your life. At the time of this publication, I'm in my early 40s. I hope that my lifetime goals span another 40+ years. Four decades is a long time! My husband and I sat down and did this exercise together once. While our Now goals were similar, our Lifetime goals were completely different! Our ideas of when, where, and how to retire were complete opposites. I love traveling, and he would be thrilled to cut his lawn and tinker in his garage because he's already traveled a lot during his life. To each their own, it's good to know what makes us both tick. Some examples of lifetime goals could be:

- Big trips

- Retire at 65

- Start a non-profit

- Sell the business

- Give the children a down payment for a home

- Buy a second vacation home to "snow bird" someplace warm

- Become a silent partner in a startup

It's hard to know exactly how much you will need for some of these lifetime goals. Inflation and changes in life will all affect how much these will cost you at the end of the day. For now, make your best guess.

Big trips	$40,000 per trip
Retire at 65	$100,000 a year for living expenses
Start a non-profit	$20,000 startup expenses
Sell the business	30% for taxes + 10% professional fees
Give the children a down payment for a home	$50,000
Buy a second vacation home to "snow bird" someplace warm	$400,000
Become a silent partner in a startup	$100,000

Remember to do this exercise with your partner if you have one. Try to complete the activity separately before comparing answers. Where do your goals align? What goals are completely different from each other?

LEGACY GOALS

Your last bucket of goals is your Legacy goals. You want to achieve these goals after your lifetime. Think long and hard about this category of goals. I break my Legacy goals down even further into family or community, but you could imagine your Legacy goals however you like. What do you want people to remember you as when you leave this earth? What do you want your family to say or do when you're gone? Do you want to leave any dollars behind to further these missions? If so, how much?

Many of my clients are working to build their empire, disrupt an industry, change the world, or challenge the status quo, the legacy they want to leave. Everyone is different. Everyone wants to be remembered uniquely. You probably have a good idea of what type of legacy you want to leave in this world. Write it down. If you know a dollar amount for this long-term goal, write that down too. We'll visit this topic at the end of the book in greater detail. Your legacy is the driving force behind what you do every single day. Without this long-term goal in your sights, it can be easy to get sidetracked, wasting time and other resources. Your legacy is the most critical aspect of this book, which is why we save the best for last.

Chapter 2

Financial Statements: Interpreting Your Numbers

I know your deep, dark secret, and I don't think any less of you! You don't know what some of these basic financial terms mean, and you're afraid to ask at the risk of sounding dumb, uneducated, or unqualified. You surpassed the million-dollar revenue mark, but your imposter syndrome comes out hard when discussing money. You nod and pretend you know everything, but you're faking it. After all, you're the boss because you're more of a "big picture" thinker than a numbers person. It's OK; I got you! No one expects you to have a Ph.D. in economics, but you need to know the basics. This chapter will discuss the fundamental financial statements you need to know, why, and how to use them daily.

Always remember that you want to see your business through the eyes of a prospective buyer. Looking at your company this way will allow you to be objective in many decisions. A buyer will always want to see the financial statements first. "Show me the money!"

Why do you think buyers are interested in a company's financial statements? Because you can't lie with the numbers. Knowing your numbers means knowing where you are right now, where you were in the past, and where you are going. GAAP stands for "Generally Accepted Accounting Principles," a U.S. standard accounting method to prevent fraud and other nasty things from happening. GAAP arose from the 1929 stock market crash to govern corporate financial reporting.[6] Remember the days of the Enron and Arthur Anderson accounting fraud schemes?[7] They fudged GAAP on their financial statements, and as you know, it ended poorly.

First, financial statements show you the current state of affairs of the business.

What's your managerial oversight like?

Is your business efficient regarding debt, operating costs, or personnel?

Is there any room for improvement?

Managing your numbers wisely means that dollars are well-spent.

Financial statements tell your company's history.

Have you ever compared the historical economic trends in your business? Compare your numbers today to the last quarter, year, or five years ago. Your numbers tell the story of your business. Many investors and lenders like to look at your historical numbers. It paints a picture of you as a risk taker and profit generator.

Planning is the last and most important reason to examine your financial statements. A client of mine knew she was at a crossroads in her business. She wanted to hire two new employees, but she needed to see if she had the budget to do so. We looked at the historical data in her financial systems with a magnifier, and she explained what the various trends meant. She wove in a story throughout the numbers, and I could see her

---

[6] https://efinancemanagement.com/financial-accounting/us-gaap

[7] https://www.hg.org/legal-articles/the-fallout-of-arthur-andersen-and-enron-on-the-legal-landscape-of-american-accounting-31277

passion for the business. After looking at her current ratios, we concluded that two new hires would be possible, but only after some time. Because of the seasonality of her revenue streams, she had some work to do.

This business owner decided to focus on the two primary revenue-producing services, add a productized service to her menu, and then see where she was. Her planning meant she should stop a service that was losing her money. While it was scary initially to admit that she no longer provided this service, it freed her and the team up to focus on what made the most money. In addition to adding two new employees, she opened a second location a year later. All this was possible because she understood her finances and could use that information as a powerful tool in her toolbelt.

When you look at your finances, you'll see where small changes in your operations can have a significant impact, either for the better or for the worse. Do you foresee a looming economic recession in the future? Are your material prices increasing? Are you thinking of raising your prices or selling more units? How much product do you need to make next year? What technology should you implement into your processes?

Right now, go ahead and log into your accounting system. Many business owners use QuickBooks, but you can use whatever system you like. You'll find the following financial statements under the *Reports* tab. In QuickBooks, you can add a yellow star to the report name to make it a favorite. Doing so will save time next month when you log in and try remembering the names of the reports. Just gold-star it for future reference.

 Then head over to www.growthconsultingfirm.com/resources. You may use this template as a reference or change it as desired.

PROFIT & LOSS STATEMENT

The first and most powerful statement is your P&L, also known as the Profit and Loss or Income Statement. It's a summary of where you stand financially at a moment in time. You still need to examine the other statements because you can't survive on this document alone. The P&L will show you only part of the picture and could be misleading if used alone. However, your P&L should appear at your team meeting at least once a month because it will summarize everything you did the previous month. I don't believe that GAAP makes it easy for you, as the business owner, to know what's happening here. Sometimes I joke and say that the "P&L lies." The net income at the bottom of each column doesn't necessarily match what's in the bank account. So don't feel ashamed if you look at your net operating income for last month and don't know where that money went. Mismatched P&Ls and bank account balances are very common,

ABC Company, LLC
Profit & Loss Statement
September 1-30, 2023

	Amount	Amount	
Sales	$500,000		
Cost of Goods Sold	$200,000		
Gross Profit		**$300,000**	
Operating Expenses			Operating
Advertising	($20,000)		
Rent	($15,000)		
Payroll taxes	($5,000)		
Salaries & Wages	($60,000)		
Other operating expenses	($9,000)		
Total Operating Expenses		($109,000)	
Net Operating Income		**$191,000**	
Non-operating Income			Non-operating
Revenue from Interest	$7,500		
Non-operating Expenses			
Interest paid on debt	($1,200)		
Net Non-Operating Income		**$6,300**	
Net Profit/Loss		**$197,300**	

Your P&L shows things like revenue earned, not necessarily cash received. It's also usually on an "accrual" basis, not a cash-in, cash-out basis. *Accrual* means that you invoiced work, but payment is outstanding. Don't think of your P&L as a cash statement. Think of your P&L as a statement that can help you analyze what's happening; that's the gold mine. You should know your P&L inside and out every day, all day. Make a point to look at this treasure trove during your monthly financial routine.

 If you don't have a monthly financial routine, there's an online checklist called the Admin Day Checklist at www.growthconsultingfirm.com/resources.

BALANCE SHEET

Now let's look at your balance sheet. This statement shows the relationship between your accounts at a single moment. The balance sheet is another document that shows a static "snapshot" of your business based on liquidity order. In other words, your assets most easily converted to cold, hard cash is first. The assets that take longer to convert to cash are last. For example, selling a CD is easy (although selling before maturity may not be wise). It's more challenging to sell a piece of real estate. Your balance sheet is the primary measure of the wealth of the business, but this differs from the value of your business. The reason is that your balance sheet doesn't show other assets like your "goodwill," land appreciation, brand name, sweat, blood, and tears, plans, competitive advantages, vendor contracts, customer contracts, employees, and more.

On the left, you'll list your assets and equity, the positive values. You'll list all your liabilities and the negative values on the right. At the bottom, each side should add up to the same number. The sides should *balance* each other, so they call it the *balance sheet*.

It would help if you also did this at least once a year for your personal life, usually around tax time. For a net worth template, visit www.growthconsultingfirm.com/resources.

You may be pleasantly surprised at how your net worth might continue to increase, even during economic turmoil. One of my clients was having a couple of bad years. One of her parents passed away, her business profits were struggling, and her marriage was on the rocks.

Her stress, to make matters worse, was taking a toll on her health. She was struggling to find peace and anything that made her smile. We kept track of her net worth over the past few years. One day, we sat down for an annual update meeting. Neither of us could have predicted that this simple exercise would have the benefit it provided, but I've been a personal fan of this activity ever since. When we examined how her net worth had increased during the past couple of years, she cried happy tears of joy. While money can't buy happiness, it did bring just a moment of positivity during an otherwise difficult time.

Your Amazing Company
Balance Sheet
Ending September 30, 2023

ASSETS			LIABILITIES & SHAREHOLDERS' EQUITY	
Current assets			Current Liabilities	
	Cash and equivalents	$565,000	Accounts payable	$30,000
	Accounts receiveable	$71,000	Credit Card	$20,000
	Inventory	$15,000	**Total current liabilities**	**$50,000**
	Total current assets	**$651,000**		
			Long-term debt	$120,000
Property & Equipment				
	Land	$644,000	**Total liabilities**	**$170,000**
	Buildings	$200,000		
	Equipment	$55,000	**Shareholders' Equity**	
			Common Stock	$15,000
Total assets		**$1,550,000**	Additional Paid-in capital	$65,000
			Retained Earnings	$150,000
			Total Shareholder's Equity	**$230,000**
			Total Liabilities & Shareholders' Equity	**$400,000**

CASH FLOW STATEMENT

The sister statement to your P&L is the cash flow statement. This report is the second most important financial statement because "Cash is King."

Your Business
Statement of Cash Flows
Ending September 30, 2023

Cash Flow from Operations	
Cash receipts from	
Customers	$475,000
Other Operations	
Cash paid for	
Wage expenses	($122,000)
Interest and taxes	($17,000)
Inventory purchases	($18,500)
Net Cash from Operations	**$317,500**
Cash Flow from Investing	
Cash receipts from	
Sales of property & equipment	$5,000
Cash paid for	
Purchase of property & equipment	($10,000)
Net Cash from Investing	**($5,000)**
Cash Flow from Financing	
Cash receipts from	
Borrowing	$5,000
Cash paid for	
Repayment of loans	($7,000)
Net Cash from Investing	**($2,000)**
Net Cash Flow for Month	**$310,500**

As a buyer, you want to know how your cash flow is doing. Nothing else matters if your cash flow is tight. You may have a giant contract paid to you next quarter, but you might need to pay your bills this month to capture that new contract. You must carefully manage your cash flow to stay afloat. This concept was pivotal in the spring of 2020. Some of the first rounds of PPP loans during the global pandemic did not go to small business owners. Instead, some of the first rounds of PPP loans went to large corporations with the staff, banking relationships, and consultants to get the paperwork together and apply for the loan.

Unfortunately, some small businesses needed the first round of PPP loans because they did not have the *cash flow* and resources to withstand a lockdown, even for a few days. These small businesses also needed basic financial knowledge to quickly and readily generate their documents and statements. They needed more staff, banking relationships, and consultants. Because of this void, many small businesses did not get the first round of PPP loans and therefore went out of business in weeks. This ultimately meant those owners could not use their business to help fund their retirement but would instead need to start over, go without, or get a full-time job elsewhere.

> **"Finance without strategy is just numbers,**
> **and strategy without finance is just dreaming."**
> **— E. Faber**

Now that you know the three fundamental statements, let's put it all together. As a small business owner, you have a finger on the pulse of your company's fiscal health. But can you pinpoint the fiscal pains or the muscles? We will do an "instant assessment" of the overall health of your business. After this exercise, you can determine whether anything needs to change how you do business. You may not like what you see, but rest assured that small changes significantly affect your finances. You must track the following four questions every month.

 Visit https://www.growthconsultingfirm.com/resources for a downloadable copy of your Scorecard Template. Remember that I am at your side through this whole process. Watch my video on the scorecard template if you are a visual learner (like me).

SCORECARD & INSTANT ASSESSMENT

#1 – Can you pay your bills?

Grab your balance sheet. This ratio is the liquidity or current asset ratio in financial terms. Think of the word liquidity as amount of cash.

Liquidity = Current Assets ÷ Current Liabilities

The word "current" means 12 months. A current asset can convert to cash within a year, like accounts payable or equivalent instruments. A current liability is anything you need to pay within a year (credit cards and accounts payable). Your answer means you have $x of cash to pay every $1.00 of bills. Many consider a range of $1.50 to $2.50 conservative, and a range of $0.50 to $1.00 is healthy. Having too much debt that you need to repay within 12 months is dangerous during economic downturns.

For example,

$101,000 ÷ $50,000 = $2.02

This company has $2.02 to pay for every $1.00 in bills. I would consider this a conservative (good) liquidity ratio.

Remember the story about the PPP loans? Some businesses that struggled through this period had low liquidity ratios, meaning they didn't have the means to pay their bills, and then the cash reserves ran out. I encourage my clients to keep their liquidity ratios conservative because you never know when something will cause you to use your cash unexpectedly. Remember that one month of low liquidity doesn't mean you're managing your cash poorly. But because you now look at your liquidity every month, you can watch for any trends or long histories of low liquidity.

So, what do you do if you have more bills than cash? The obvious answer is to increase your net profits and decrease your bills. Bring in more cash, or stop spending money, honey! You can also reduce your accounts receivables time to collect your client payments sooner rather than later. Another strategy might be to get a long-term loan during a debt consolidation and change your short-term debt into a long-term debt obligation. How ever you decide to fix this ratio, make sure this is a talking point on your monthly finance agenda.

#2 – How risky is your business?

Another calculation for your balance sheet is the Debt-to-Equity ratio. This ratio will show the relationship between your company's equity and liabilities (leverage). It's your banker's favorite ratio and among the first things they will look at if you ever go to them asking for a loan.

Debt to Equity Ratio = Total Liabilities ÷ Equity

For our example, Debt to Equity = $170,000 ÷ $230,000 = 0.739

The answer means that this example company has $0.73 of debt for every dollar of equity. So, if you sold your equity off, you would have more than enough money to pay back your debt obligations. You want this number to stay less than 1.0. If your total liabilities exceed your equity, you are slowly going bankrupt.

In 2008, the banks in the United States were in crisis. I remember this time well. In essence, many banks didn't have the reserves to back up the money they were loaning to people. Nowadays, there are stricter requirements for banks. They can only loan out what they have. Banks must stick to certain debt levels the federal government regularly tests.

Companies during this time were living large. They had lavish parties, big contracts, and life was good. The truth was that these companies had leveraged themselves from head to toe. Companies had more debt than equity in the company. Because the banks were in crisis, they called in their notes overnight. If you had a loan from the bank for a million dollars, the bank wanted their payment by 8:00 a.m. the next day. If you couldn't pay, then you defaulted on the loan. If you defaulted on the loan, you were in financial trouble. Overnight. It wasn't pretty for the banks or the businesses.

The moral of the story is never to take on more debt than you can readily pay back. If you want to take out a new loan or feel obligated to pay it down, pay attention to this ratio. I'm not saying that debt is bad. Debt can be really good! Sometimes, debt can propel a business to the next level using leverage. An owner uses someone else's money to invest in a new product or service, expand the business or hire a new employee, and gain a larger return on investment. However, ensure you get a higher ROI (return on investment) than you pay in interest. You need to ensure you can reasonably repay the debt if your gamble doesn't pay off.

For those of you who want to fix your Debt-to-Equity ratio, here are some ideas to implement:

Manage growth: Wait to spend your money before you earn it. Companies can get into trouble if they start spending before they have a consistent cash flow. Let a few months of growth sink in before you act on any new plans.

Pay down your debt: I hope this is an obvious answer for you. If you want to increase your Debt-to-Equity ratio, plan to pay down your debt as much as possible. Doing so will lower your ratio.

#3 - Are you profitable?

This is my favorite question to ask business owners. I usually get a deer-in-the-headlights answer. Many think they are profitable but aren't sure if they are correct.

"**Revenue is vanity, but profit is sanity**"
— **Alan Miltz**

It's test time! Grab your P&L so we can look at your profit margin. You can see precisely how much of each dollar of revenue actually becomes profit.

$$Gross\ Profit\ Margin\ (GPM) = \frac{(Revenue - COGS)}{Revenue}\ x\ 100$$

Or

$$Net\ Profit\ Margin\ (NPM) = \frac{(Revenue - COGS - Operating\ Expenses)}{Revenue}\ x\ 100$$

COGS = "Cost of Goods Sold"

In our example, GPM = ($500k-$200k) ÷ $500k x100 = 60% profit before paying expenses.

Gross profit margin is the percentage of revenue that exceeds the cost of goods sold. In other words, this is the "cushion" you have after making or selling a product. This sounds pretty good, right? Focus on your gross profit margin if you make or sell a product.

However, net profit margin can be quite different. In this example, we have NPM = (500k-200k-250k) ÷ 500k x 100 = 10%. Your net profit margin result might be pretty different from the gross margin. If you were dancing and celebrating with your GPM, you might not be so excited right now, looking at 10 percent or less. Note that if you are a service provider, you want to focus on your NET profit margin instead of your GROSS profit margin. How much do you have after you pay all your overhead?

Measuring profit is challenging; you get different answers, depending on whom you ask. A banker will measure profit differently from an equity analyst, who will answer differently from an M&A attorney. Various consultants will use measurements like the profit and loss statement, gross (or net) profit margin, return on invested capital, shareholder's equity, EBITDA (Earnings Before Interest, Taxes, Deductions and Amortization), or simple revenue.

The secret here is how you, as the business owner, want to measure your profitability. Start with your profit margins and one or a few other areas to analyze regularly. Compare it to your competitors to see where you stand. Then establish a goal to aim for a monthly profitability target and always measure yourself to see what your projection was and how it compared to your actual numbers. Be sure to back up your assumptions and reasonings to communicate your plans to other stakeholders, from employees to investors. As the owner of your company, you get to set the tone and targets.

Head over to www.growthconsultingfirm.com/resources to download an example of a forecasted budget vs. actual budget spreadsheet.

We are going to focus on the net profit margin for the purposes of this book. If you have gone through this exercise, and your margins are not where you want them to be, do not stress. Let's talk about simple but effective ways to improve your profit margins. Below are some ideas that you can take back to your company and adapt for your purposes. These four simple activities could help you improve your margins instantly. Remember that even small changes can significantly impact the bottom line.

1. Cut unnecessary fluff!

I make clients do an exercise that is tedious and something they all hate. I call them "financial burpees." It's arduous, but it's really good for you. We completely download the last 12 months of expenses from payroll to staplers. I make them print it out and take a red marker to cross out all the costs they need to cut in their business. I encourage you to try this as well. If it's helpful, break this list into types of expenses and vendors or sort by other criteria. Then assign a team member to each expense list and come back to compare notes. Some areas to look for include:

- Subscriptions for services no longer in use
- "Bad" purchasing decisions to never repeat again
- Accidental owner expenses charged to the business
- Fraud or misused expenses charged by an employee or contractor
- Unknown expenses — track them down
- Expenses that are too high — could you get them cheaper?
- And more!

This exercise is meant to bring awareness to your business operations. As the owner, you should know every dollar spent, and every dollar spent should yield an acceptable ROI (return on investment). If you find that some expenses are not serving you anymore, it might be time to reconsider their place in your company. There is a better use for that mighty dollar that could bring you a better return. Think about all the plans you might have waiting in the wings: a new hire, a new piece of equipment, or expansion plans. Completing this exercise is a great way to find money — fast and cheap! You don't need to get approval from a bank; you need to stop spending in this area.

You're welcome; I've just improved your profit margins overnight!

2. Leverage technology to help your operations.

A hundred years ago, many women would have loved to become a receptionist or secretary. Today, I have a human voice recording that answers my VOIP phone line. I receive an automatic email when someone leaves me a voicemail. I also use transcription software to turn my video conferences or voice notes into a written document. Technology can be a great tool to lower costs and increase efficiency. If this is something that you use in your business, be sure to do all the research and due diligence on the tool before you implement it. Look at security measures, backup processes, and even how they use your customer's information. Read the privacy policy. Look at the fees carefully. Artificial intelligence or any technology cannot genuinely replace the human component of the business. However, until that day comes, I am happy to leverage technology where I can.

3. Over-deliver customer service for the best results.

Small businesses have a competitive advantage in this area. Think of the last time you called a major national brand's toll-free number. You probably had a problem you need to solve. Maybe you needed to rebook airline tickets. Perhaps you needed to return an item, or maybe you needed to ask a question about a warranty on a product that you own. Did you call an 800 number? Were you transferred? Did you get a chance to talk to a human? Was that human in the same country? Could they answer your question to your satisfaction? The last time I called an 800 number, I waited to talk to a human. Four transfers later, and my problem still remained. I had to call back several times.

Small businesses have an advantage because they can make this experience better for their clients than large corporations. Small companies can own the customer's problem and deliver the best customer service experience possible. Your customer's problem may not be your fault. It might not have anything to do with you. But if a customer calls to complain or get a solution to a problem, you can do something about it because you own the resources and supply chain to solve their problem.

How does customer service improve profit margins? Pleasing a customer leads to better brand reputation, increased goodwill, more referrals, more sales, and ultimately better margins. The best part is that it doesn't have to cost you any money to deliver the best customer service. Begin by implementing policies within your company that would make you come back for more assistance. Increase your profit margins by ensuring you over-deliver the best customer service possible.

4. Focus on what makes the most money in your business, then scale that product or service.

Take a look at which product or service has the highest margins. Put all your time and energy into that offering. Consider removing any product or service with a low margin.

First, start with what the buyer will pay for your product or service. Many entrepreneurs start with their own cost, then mark it up. For example, pretend you are a store owner selling pens and pencils. It costs you wholesale $0.50 to buy a pen, and you mark it up to $1.00 retail price to your customers. Likewise, it costs you $0.25 to purchase pencils wholesale, and you mark it up to $0.50 to sell to your customers.

	Your Cost	Selling Price	Profit
Pen	$0.50	$1.00	$0.50
Pencil	$0.25	$0.50	$0.25

Now let's say that you surveyed past, present, and potential customers. You asked them how much they would pay for a pen or a pencil. You learned that customers don't want pencils anymore. No one uses them. No one cares about pencils anymore. Plus, the pencil that you offer has a terrible eraser. The survey results said customers would only pay $0.10 for a pencil. Yikes! That means you are *losing money* by providing the pencil in your store.

On the flip side, everyone seems to love the pens you sell. They write smoothly, upside down, and even in the rain. The grip is excellent, and the survey results said people would pay $5.00 per pen. Wowza! That means that you have been undercharging this entire time!

	Your Cost	New Selling Price	New Profit
Pen	$0.50	$5.00	$4.50
Pencil	$0.25	$0.10	-$0.15

What are you going to do, now armed with this new information?

My hope is that you…

- Stop selling pencils
- Increase the retail price of your pens

Rather than be known as the store that sells pens and pencils, it may be time to pivot the business. Perhaps it's time to be known as the "World's Best Pen Shop"! Don't worry about being all things to all people. And if you are a lover of pencils, that's OK. You can still buy personal pencils, but you don't need to have them in your business. The pen and pencil story is a simplified metaphor. I've encountered many owners who are reluctant to give up a dying service because it's close to their hearts. I know it isn't easy, but remember you are trying to sell your company someday. Your business buyer will not care how much you love pencils. If the product or service no longer works within your business, you must be brave enough to recognize this trend and move on.

#4 - Are you compensated as an owner?

I'll bet you didn't start a business to work until midnight every day, pour all your 401(k) money into the startup costs, and not get a single dime back. When I ask my clients why they started their companies, they tell me stories of wanting to retire on their terms, control the inputs and the outputs, make a difference in the world, or even fund their lifestyle. When I speak to women owners, at least one or two in the group always say that they don't pay themselves much because they are "reinvesting in the business." I call this total bull poop because I know the reason they pay themselves last is that they're in financial distress. They don't know how to manage their money, and because of that, they don't sleep well at night.

Think of all the many hats you wear as an owner. You probably do all the hiring, sales and marketing, client service, bookkeeping, and make long-term strategic decisions. How much would you pay them if you were to pay four people to do these jobs individually? Compare this number to what you pay yourself.

The IRS tests S-corporations to see if the owner compensates herself with a reasonable salary. Try this exercise to gauge a reasonable range for your salary, even if you are not taking the S-corporation election with your taxes. Many accountants cite the "40 percent rule." but I don't think that's enough. Are you paying yourself a regular and fair salary as a business owner? Are you compensated fairly for the

1. Time that you spend in the business

2. The experience and certifications that you have

3. Comparable wages with the industry?

I hope the answers are *yes*! If not, we need to examine your financial statements to determine why your pay is too low. You need to fix this line item as soon as possible. You may need more time to fix it but set a goal you want to work toward. Don't count on distributions at the end of the year or "owner draws" to make up for your salary. Taxing authorities tax distributions at the capital gains rate of maybe 15 percent if you're the owner of an S-corporation. The IRS taxes your salary in your income tax bracket, perhaps 22 percent to 32 percent. You can see why the IRS is very interested in ensuring that S-corporations get this right.

Right now, let's look at how you pay yourself from the business. Get a pen and answer these questions from what you already know of your financials.

What is your annual compensation from the business?

Salary _____

Distribution _____

What job functions do you provide for the business?

_____

If you hired someone to do your job(s), how much would that cost the business?

_____

What would you like your compensation to be in 12 months?

Salary _____

Distribution _____

What must you do to get to this compensation goal?

_____

Unfortunately I know many business owners of multi-million dollar companies (in revenue) that pay themselves barely a livable wage. My goal is to get you to a place where you can sustain a comfortable lifestyle and grow your company wisely and responsibly.

Chapter 3

Setup: A Legal Foundation

Legal Structure

Having the correct legal structure for your business today will determine your options for sale tomorrow. If you have the wrong legal structure set up, you may be surprised that you have a limited exit when it comes time to leave the business. Sometimes founders think that it's not a big deal or that they'll get around to setting up a corporation eventually.

You want the correct legal structure in place from the start for three reasons. First, protect your family. If you have a disgruntled client or an employee that gets injured, they can come after you and your livelihood. You could be liable personally and professionally for any damage done. If you are a sole proprietor, the injured party could seek restitution, including your home. What would then become of your family?

Second, protect your business. The correct legal structure can give you additional protections, whether it's a partnership, LLC, or C-corp. You can also protect your business assets, employees, and clients.

Third, although many more reasons exist, having the correct legal structure at the start will help facilitate a successful sale. You'll attract more venture capitalists, private equity partners, and buyers. However, having the proper legal structure for your business is paramount and frequently founders push it to the wayside. Thankfully, you are no longer a founder; you are the CEO of a growing company. Ensure you seek a legal professional to walk you through your various options. Please do not constitute this book as legal advice.

Banking Structure

Please take away at least two things from this book; first, to ensure you have a *valid* will, and second, to separate your bank accounts from your personal and business money. If you are a business owner, you should have all your revenue go into your business checking account, and all your business expenses come out of your business checking account. Do not pay business expenses with your personal account, and do not pay personal expenses with your business account.

Benefits of separating your business from your personal expenses:

- Start building a relationship with a local bank or credit union
- Easier to do your bookkeeping and financial analysis
- Therefore, it's cheaper and faster to do your taxes!
- You stay out of trouble with the IRS

And, ultimately we don't have to *recast* your financials when we try to sell your business, which is very expensive and time-consuming. Recasting is the process of adding back expenses that a new owner wouldn't necessarily pay for in the daily operations of the business. These are typically owner discretionary expenses like having a relative on the payroll, expensing a personal vehicle, and the like.

Consequences of commingling your personal and business accounts

- You adapt to the business paying for personal expenses, and your business becomes a "lifestyle" business that will ultimately liquidate only at your retirement because it is unsalable.

- You start doing mental accounting, moving money back and forth between accounts in your mind. Trust me; no matter how good you are at math, this is a bad idea.

- You must pay a professional a lot of money to clean up this mental accounting mess.

- Your filed taxes could miss significant deductions or credits

- Your P&L and B/S, and CFS are all screwed up, so you can't analyze your finances, you can't make sound strategic decisions, and you sure as heck can't pivot fast enough if there's a disaster.

- You miss opportunities.

- You overpay.

If you are in this boat and do not separate your financial transactions, don't worry! I know this can be overwhelming, but it's better to clean it up now rather than later. You must roll up your sleeves for a few months of work, but I promise it's worth the pain.

Here's the bare minimum of what you need:

1. Business Checking Account (Revenue in + Expenses out)

Deposit the money into this account when a customer pays you. When you set up payment for a vendor, whether software, supplies, contract workers, insurance, or rent, the money should come from this account.

Note: A word about signers. While you may be the primary person paying the bills and making all the financial decisions, you need a second person on each account. Make sure it's someone you trust, and make sure that you check each other's activities. Fraud happens frequently within small businesses. You need a second person because you want to go on vacation over a payroll period. Or, what if you end up in the hospital and your employees cannot get paid? Get a trusted secondary signer on your accounts but verify everything.

2. Business Savings Account(s) = (Quarterly taxes + emergency fund + excess cash + sinking funds)

You might have one or several savings accounts. The number of accounts depends on your processes, personality, and business structure.

Working with your tax preparer, calculate the estimated taxes you owe this year. Make quarterly tax payments through the IRS online system. (You can do this yourself, or the tax preparer can do it for you.) This is not an optional task, and the IRS will penalize you for grossly underpaying your taxes every quarter.

You also want at least two months of operating expenses saved in this account for an emergency. I'm talking about minimum monthly expenses to keep the lights on and your employees paid. What does it cost to run your business for one month? Multiply that cost by the number of months you need in the bank. For example, if you are a seasonal business, you may want four months of expenses set aside for an emergency. If you have a slow year because of a pandemic or recession, can you survive? Some people may only need two months but feel more comfortable with three. So, multiply your minimum essential operating expenses by three, which becomes your emergency fund goal. Get this funded 100 percent as soon as possible.

If you have a buy-sell agreement, you want to establish a "sinking fund" reserve to buy out your partner.

Sales commissions should also go into this savings account so that you are satisfied with the payment you owe your sales team.

Any excess cash you may have left over also goes into this or another business savings account. The extra cash will remain here until you need it for an expansion or investment.

3. Business Credit Card

Start building credit in the business name, even if it's only a little initially. People only need credit scores and history to use credit one day. Credit can be a great way to grow your company if done correctly. Start with a small amount and open the cheapest credit card account that you can find. Don't worry about the rewards. Trust me; no millionaire ever got rich from credit card rewards. After you open this account, put small purchases on the card, but pay them off monthly. You'll build credit very quickly this way. Once or twice a year, call and ask for a credit line increase without having them check your credit history. Sometimes credit card companies can increase your available credit this way, and sometimes they can't. It doesn't hurt to ask.

4. Personal Checking Account (Salary in from your business checking account + personal expenses out)

If you aren't already, pay yourself a monthly salary starting from the last day of your first month in business. It might be a small salary but get into the habit of paying yourself. The IRS doesn't have a rule on how much you need to pay yourself or your employees if you are a sole proprietorship or an LLC. However, certain S- and C-corporation rules require the owner's pay is a "fair and reasonable" salary before any distributions. I pinned my first owner's salary check to my bulletin board to remind me where I came from. It was a check I wrote out to myself for $6.42, not even enough to buy lunch. Paying yourself a regular paycheck is a good habit for many reasons.

5. Personal Savings Account (Emergency fund + excess cash)

Much like your business, your personal life also needs an emergency fund. Traditional advice tells you to have six months' monthly personal expenses in your emergency fund. But this number differs for each family's circumstance, temperament, and economic environment. Are you more comfortable with nine months of rent in your fund? Does it only take four weeks to find a job if your company failed because you are in a highly competitive career field? Does a looming recession require you to have seven or eight months of cash? Make a goal for this emergency fund, then start putting excess cash into it for a rainy day. If you are a good saver, you can put even more into this fund to build up an opportunity to invest in something else one day. The world is your oyster!

6. Tax Setup

For Pete's sake, please get a professional bookkeeper and tax preparer.

You can maybe do your bookkeeping the first year if you are disciplined and teach yourself how to use an accounting tool like QuickBooks. You can learn by watching many YouTube videos or taking a course. After your humble bootstrapping beginnings, hire a knowledgeable and experienced bookkeeper. The bookkeeper categorizes every expense correctly, allowing the tax preparer to file your taxes correctly. The bookkeeper can also reconcile your accounts within the software monthly, enabling you to pull the three crucial financial statements monthly — balance sheet, profit and loss and statement of cash flows. Please don't skimp on this expense because you need to know your numbers regularly.

Being diligent about your bookkeeping and taxes will save you more money and heartache than if you had done it incorrectly.

I can't tell you how many stories I've heard of small business owners who hired their "husband's niece's friend's friend who used to do bookkeeping once or twice for someone's farm" who ended up embezzling money from the company or messed everything up because they simply didn't know what they were doing. Small companies are much more vulnerable to fraud than large corporations because many small business owners rely on favors and service exchanges. Don't be a statistic. Get a professional bookkeeper, preferably someone who does only bookkeeping. You also want to ask your bookkeeper for monthly or quarterly financial statements.

A good tax preparer, whether a CPA or an Enrolled Agent, is worth their weight in gold. You want someone who ideally gives you good advice and education through the process and will look out for all the credits and deductions that may apply to your business. Not all tax preparers and bookkeepers are the same, so make sure that you look for service providers who will be your partner, not just see you as another transaction. You want strategy and substance.

Case Study: The Fast-growing Owners

Meet Scott & Shelly: This lovely couple has a very humble background in the education sector. They were both teachers at a Title 1 public school for many years and have a heart for public service. Scott and Shelly have two kids, an aspiring scientist and an avid football player. However, once they started having kids, Shelly decided to quit teaching and stay home to homeschool. Scott took on a side gig as a construction worker to make some extra income.

Fast forward seven years, and Scott now owns a construction company specializing in providing a service no one else does in Montana. He works as the foreman, procurement officer, and training manager, to name a few of his jobs. Shelly also now works in the company as bookkeeper, receptionist, client service manager, human resources, and more. They currently have six employees and make over $ 7 million in revenue, twice as much as last year and the previous year. Their company is growing faster than they know how to keep up.

Scott & Shelly's Goals: To find balance in their work and life. Scott and Shelly want to spend more time with their children and family. They also want to take care of their current employees and one day sell the business.

Scott & Shelly's Obstacles: Scott and Shelly need more expertise to run a larger company. They've never managed employees and are struggling to find the right people to help. Despite their quick rise to success, they only take out enough money from their company to pay the bills. They don't have a will, power of attorney, or other safeguards. On paper, their business is hugely profitable. But their company is unfortunately not tax efficient, meaning they are paying more taxes than they should. Their business is also sitting on too much cash that they could distribute to the owners or reinvest into the company. Scott and Shelly have nine different personal life insurance policies sold to them over time by several other financial advisors. They are paying too much in premiums, and the policies are no longer applicable, but they need to figure out what they need and why.

Scott's cousin has been helping with the bookkeeping over the past few years because Scott and Shelly have yet to have a chance to dedicate any energy to the books. A prospective buyer has approached them and wants to see their financial statements to make an offer. Unfortunately, it might be months before they can produce any financial report for the prospective buyer. They also need to figure out what their options are when it comes to selling their business.

Scott & Shelly's Outcome: First and foremost, I always advise my clients to get the proper estate planning documents in place. Since they have young children, it was essential to make sure their wills, POAs, and medical directives were up to date with a good estate planning attorney. We deeply investigated each insurance policy and discovered they were overpaying and underinsured. I call these policies "band-aids" because the owners thought they needed insurance at one point in time to fix a pain point, but the policies aren't cohesive.

Over time, they accumulated many Band-Aids, but they needed to find out whether the policies were still helping. By consolidating what we could, transitioning some policies into a whole life, and cashing out another to purchase a more comprehensive term policy, we ensured they had the correct protection in the event of an unforeseen circumstance. I connected them with an outsourced general manager who transformed their business in less than 12 months. They set policies and procedures into place and could finally take their first family vacation in three years. Their employee turnover went down, and their customer satisfaction improved. Working as their outsourced CFO, I taught them what to look for in their finances and how to interpret critical financial metrics.

We interviewed bookkeeping companies to find the right fit for their company and started to work closely with a CPA to transition their business into an S-corporation and take advantage of other strategies that mitigated their tax bill. Unfortunately, we uncovered multiple suspicious transactions where Scott's cousin skimmed the books and pocketed some extra cash. Still, the CPA also found thousands of dollars of unclaimed deductions and credits. Scott and Shelly now pay themselves a competitive wage and are saving for their kids' college education, retirement, and potential expansion. At the ripe old age of 45, these two have begun priming the business for sale. They want to be ready for when the right opportunity comes along.

Chapter 4

Get ready for Tax Season

Yes, the "T-word" (taxes) gives most people anxiety and heart palpitations. You don't want to go to jail for failing to pay your taxes, but you don't want to spend too much on taxes. If we go back to our history books from elementary school, do you remember why you are paying taxes? Taxes are collected by the government so that schools can buy elementary school books, pave the roads in your town, and protect your community. Politics and red tape frequently buckle these goals, but the true spirit of a tax is meant for the good of our communities. Did you know that the creators of IRS (Internal Revenue Service) tax code wrote it to *reduce* the tax burden on American citizens? I know your mind is blown! Go ahead and read that last sentence again.

The IRS makes money *internally* from its citizens, but it's for a good cause. As a business owner, you pay a lot in taxes. It might be because you must learn how to navigate the tax code legally. It's challenging to reduce your tax obligation now while you're scaling your business and later when you live off the sale of your business. It is possible to be a good citizen and reduce your tax burden within the confines of the law. We won't go over specific tax reduction strategies in this book. I aim to educate you on how to prepare for a stress-free year of taxes. We'll discuss what you need to do and know how to prepare to pay your taxes fully. When you are ready throughout the year, you save time and money at the end of the day, and you can sleep well knowing you are doing your part as a responsible citizen.

Years ago, the daughter of a business owner I worked with showed up at my office on March first. She had shoe boxes full of receipts, bills, bank statements, and other unopened mail. She said she would drop it off at her dad's accountant's office but wanted help sorting through the papers to know what she should and shouldn't keep. My hourly rate was more expensive than if they had hired a bookkeeper or in-house administrative person, but she still wanted help. It took us the better part of four hours to open envelopes, read, and sort.

She took the boxes to the accountant, but they had to file an extension. They still had to file 1099s and return to headquarters to find other documents. To their surprise, this client found out that they owed a large amount of taxes for the previous year and had to pay penalties on top of those taxes because they should have paid quarterly. Had they hired an administrative assistant throughout the year to open, scan, file, and shred, they would have been in a much better position to begin filing the taxes for the business.

Unfortunately, this is a typical story of business owners needing to be more organized for tax time. It ends up causing them much more stress and money in the end. Thankfully, you can implement an effective plan that anticipates your tax obligation!

Types of Tax Professionals

Many types of financial professionals exist in the country. If you aren't in the finance world daily, it can be difficult to distinguish between them. Small or medium-sized companies can outsource these positions to businesses specializing in these areas. While having segregated tasks might cost a little bit more, many business owners find having a different person in each position helpful. For example, having a separate bookkeeper from your tax preparer can provide checks and balances for your company that might otherwise be fertile ground for someone to take advantage of you.

I have often heard a business owner lament about hiring an internal bookkeeper who siphoned money away from the business and into their checking account. Or how a tax preparer made significant errors on the tax return, and it was when they hired a part-time CFO they found out they violated several tax codes. You want to avoid being in the position of handing over your trust only to be disappointed. Creating checks and balances will be vital to your success and save you thousands of dollars in your finances and other business areas.

There was once a very lively tax consultant on social media who got many business owners' attention by promising them "strategic" tax planning that would save them hundreds of thousands of dollars. She had a fabulous presence online and danced, drank wine, showed off her perfectly manicured nails, and made wild claims about her success. Her social media page drew lots of followers.

One client began working with me about a year into the relationship with this tax advisor. The advisor promised my client a tax reduction, quarterly check-ins, payroll services, and financial reporting. I thought her monthly fee was ridiculously high for "strategic tax planning," but she also provided payroll and bookkeeping services, so maybe the cost was worth the benefit. The tax advisor took the S-corp election for my client's LLC. The election meant the client was an LLC (limited liability company) but wanted the authorities to tax them as an S-corporation and have the business pay the self-employment taxes, not the owner.

It's completely legal to do this sort of tax planning. However, the tax consultant also said that the client should pay herself next to nothing in annual salary but instead take a large draw out of the company at the end of the year. This strategy set off major red flags for me. The IRS will tax a salary at "ordinary income" rates, which could be anywhere from 22 to 35 percent tax. The IRS taxes owner draws at capital gain rates, which are right now, 2023, anywhere from 0 percent, 15 percent, or 20 percent. If the IRS audited my client, which she was a prime candidate for, the IRS could declare that her salary was not high enough in relation to tasks she performed as a business owner. They could make her refile and pay the taxes they thought she owed, plus penalties.

I introduced this client to several other tax preparers. The one she eventually hired took a look at previous tax returns that this advisor had filed and immediately declared that the advisor had made egregious errors and set up the client for possible audits in the future. The tax advisor also made many mistakes in the bookkeeping and payroll. What the tax advisor was doing was in the "gray" area of finances, but it was also extremely short-sighted.

Declaring zero income meant that my client would have difficulty finding any lenders to give her a loan for a new house. It also meant that a potential buyer of the company would not even give her the time of day because it wasn't a profitable business. Ultimately, it cost my client so much more money to retrace her footsteps, file the correct tax return, and pay back taxes. Be cautious of the help that you find. If it sounds too good to be true, it probably is!

Bookkeeper

A bookkeeper is an individual who records the daily transactions in your books. They balance the debits (money that goes out of your accounts) and the credits (money that goes into your accounts). A bookkeeper sometimes pays the bills and collects the invoices, although not all do. No formal training is necessary, but they should know how to use software such as Gusto, Xero, or QuickBooks. Please don't hire someone cheap, like your cousin's best friend's old coworker's ex-fiancée. You may run into more problems down the road.

Accountant

An accountant can do bookkeeping services, although that is not always the best use of their time. You need an accountant with experience to reconcile your debits and credits at the end of every month. They should produce your company's financial statements and ensure the information is accurate. At a minimum, you should always get your profit and loss (aka income statement), balance sheet and statement of cash flows quarterly. Bonus points if they send you your equity statement by the end of each month. Some training is necessary to be an accountant, but they cannot sign off on your tax forms or represent you in an IRS audit.

CPA (Certified Public Accountant)

A CPA is a great friend to have in your corner. They are current on all the latest tax laws and have hopefully seen thousands of tax returns in their career. Their tax knowledge is broad and wide-ranging. They can offer you great advice because they have had extensive training and are state licensed. They can prepare your tax forms and quarterly financial reports.

Enrolled Agent

An EA is another great friend to have on your side, just like the CPA above. The only difference here is that an EA does not have a degree in accounting and has a license with the IRS on a federal level. Their expertise runs very deep when it comes to tax codes and law.

	Task	Advice	Sign Tax Form	Training	License	IRS Representation
Bookkeeper	Accurately Record Daily Financial Transactions	No	No	None Required	No	No
Accountant	Prepare Detailed Financial Reports	Yes	No	Some	No	No
CPA	Prepare Detailed Financial Reports	Yes	Yes	Extensive	State	Yes
Enrolled Agent	Prepare tax returns	Yes	Yes	Extensive	Federal	Yes

Once you have identified people to interview, there are several questions you should ask to determine their expertise. My recommendation is to interview two or three individuals at a minimum. Here are just a few sample questions to ask when hiring a tax professional:

Sample questions to ask when hiring a tax professional

- What is your experience?
- What credentials do you have?
- Who will sign my tax return?
- Who will I work with directly?
- What type of clients do you work with?
- How are your fees calculated?
- Can I ask questions throughout the year?

- What is your typical turnaround for phone calls, emails, tax forms, etc.?
- What happens if I get audited?
- What do you expect from me?
- Will you help me understand my taxes?
- Will you give me advice?
- Why should I use you?

Tax planning throughout the year

 Remember, you're not alone in all of this. I've developed resources for you to get and stay organized for taxes. For a copy of the Tax Time Checklist, visit https://www.growthconsultingfirm.com/resources.

Pro Tip: Have regular check-ins with your tax preparer throughout the year. Tell them your plans for everything. An excellent tax preparer will help you strategize to take advantage of current-year tax deductions and credits, thus saving you lots of money at the end of the year.

I had a client once purchase a large EV (Electric Vehicle) for her business, then tell me and the CPA at the end of the year that she thought she had a significant tax deduction for the company. We had to inform her that the EV did not meet the IRS criteria for the credit. Had she kept either of us in the loop before she bought the vehicle, we could have seen this issue and saved her a lot of money. It also would have been wiser for her to lease the vehicle rather than purchase it outright in her case.

Chapter 5

The Savings Waterfall

My husband joined the military when he was 18 years old. He was bright-eyed and full of hope for the future but had no idea what he was supposed to be doing regarding his money. All he knew was to spend less than he made. At the time, a great supervisor told him to put 5 percent of his paycheck into his retirement savings. The supervisor recommended that his junior members do this with their paychecks. My husband didn't know why he was supposed to do it, but he didn't question his superior. Fast forward more than two decades later, thanks to this supportive leader, he has a comfortable retirement nest egg.

He took advantage of two things: time and yield. That small portion of his very tiny paycheck at the time was not very much at all. An A1C (Airman First Class) rank barely made much more than the poverty line at the time. But his boss told him to set it and forget it. Each five percent saved adds to the last. Plus, he invested his savings into a target date fund, a mix of mutual funds that gets progressively more conservative as time reaches the target date. Each time he deposited money into the account, it would earn a yield. Then, that money would grow, and he would deposit more savings, and that money would earn a yield, and so on. In the financial world, we call this compounding. It's a beautiful thing! My husband didn't even know he was doing it and forgot about his retirement account until I asked about it years later when we married. By then, he was pleasantly surprised to see his account balance. For a 25-year-old, he felt as if he was rolling in the dough.

This chapter is about savings, specifically what order to save it, what to save in, how much to save, and so on. While you are scaling your business, saving money for the future is still important, either in case your business is nonsalable or as an addition to the proceeds from your business sale. No one can predict the future, but we can plan for multiple scenarios. Neither insurance nor good sense can mitigate everything, so it's best to overprepare by saving for your future.

A good savings plan is also a good tax strategy.

Now that you know why you should save, let's dive into the order of operations of savings. There are right and wrong ways to save in a perfect world where life goes according to plan. I will illustrate the ideal order in which you should save money. Keep in mind that life doesn't ever look like the ideal order that I will illustrate. Throw in kids, ex-partners, elderly parents, vacations, college, taxes, business opportunities, and more, and the correct order of operations goes entirely out the door. But I offer this illustration so you can see which aspects you can adopt and which ones are out of reach, even if it's temporary. Also, remember you will want to review this savings waterfall every year because life constantly changes.

 Head over to https://www.growthconsultingfirm.com/resources to grab a copy of the savings waterfall worksheet. Then, come back and follow along with the rest of the chapter.

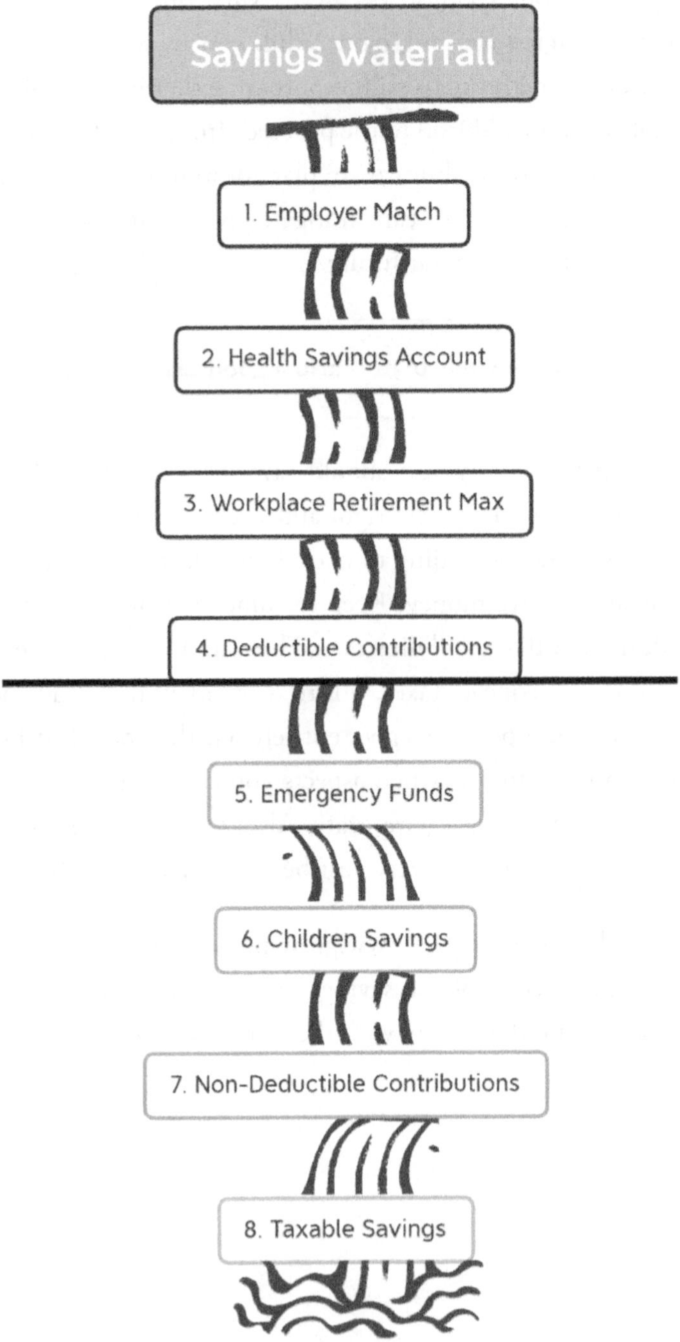
Savings Waterfall
1. Employer Match
2. Health Savings Account
3. Workplace Retirement Max
4. Deductible Contributions
5. Emergency Funds
6. Children Savings
7. Non-Deductible Contributions
8. Taxable Savings

Above the line in the waterfall graphic are what's called pre-tax savings. At the end of the year, the IRS will look at your total net revenue and income, then subtract the amount you contributed to these pre-tax accounts. You pay taxes on the remaining amount (minus other deductions and credits). When you pull money out of these accounts later in life, your tax is on the amount you take out. The financial term is "deferred tax". You defer the taxes owed on the income or revenue for a later date, ideally retirement. Clear as mud, right? Think of each category as a bucket that needs money. We start with the first bucket, fill it up, and then move to the next one.

1. EMPLOYER MATCH

If you earn any income, you are eligible to save for retirement. I'm not talking about getting your Social Security check or child support. Earned income is income from your business, job, rental property, investments, etc. Start with the employer's match if it's available to you. Many employers (but not all) offer a company match in a business-sponsored retirement plan. If this is you or your spouse, start here.

You want to contribute to this company plan to get the employer's match. It's like free money, except that it's just a part of your compensation plan. For example, your spouse's job allows them to contribute to a 401(k) plan. Their employer said they would match all of the first three percent of his salary. That means your spouse should contribute at least three percent of his salary to his 401(k) plan or 403(b), or other plans offered.

You as a business owner and with your own earned income should consult a financial advisor to see what type of retirement plan best suits your situation this year. She can tell you how much you can contribute to this plan because the IRS updates its limits every calendar year. Check out the latest updates on www.irs.gov, and ensure you have a professional to walk you through this exercise. If you have a solo 401(k) plan for your small business, ensure that your company contributes the employer's maximum amount. Set aside that monthly or once a quarter to contribute to your plan.

2. HEALTH SAVINGS ACCOUNT

An HSA is very different from an FSA (Flexible Spending Account). An FSA is a use it or lose it type of account sponsored by an employer for additional employee benefits.

I'm talking about the Health Savings Account, a compelling savings tactic. You contribute pre-tax dollars for health expenses. Again, check out the IRS website for the maximum contribution you can make if you are single or have a family.

Invest your contributions so the money grows over time, compounding your savings. When health expenses come up, you can reimburse yourself out of the HSA (please keep your receipts for tax time). The money you pull out is not taxable or even tax-deferred. As of the date of this publishing, you can even use the funds for long-term care and final burial expenses, then leave the remaining account balance to your heirs and beneficiaries. The HSA is a powerful little account.

Fill it up every year if you are eligible. And, if you can afford it, don't use the account to reimburse yourself for medical expenses this year. You can reimburse yourself, but you can also leave the money in the account and let it grow. Here's the "big but." You must qualify for the HSA through a high-deductible health care insurance plan. My family has Tricare, a low-deductible government-sponsored program, so unfortunately, we can't have an HSA. But if you're eligible, you can open one up through many banks or brokerage firms. Compare fees and reimbursement processes. Also, make sure you tell your accountant or tax preparer.

3. WORKPLACE RETIREMENT MAX

Return to your workplace retirement account and put the maximum contribution into your account. Let's go back and talk about your spouse's 401(k) plan. Let's say his employer only matched three percent of his salary, but he can contribute up to 12 percent. (The IRS determines this maximum amount annually. Ask your tax preparer or financial advisor about your circumstances.) In this case, your spouse will want to contribute 12 percent of his salary. It's alright if he can't do all 12 percent right now. Because of inflation or extra vacations, he might only be able to afford to contribute ten percent of his salary right now. Make it a goal to fill up this bucket as soon as possible.

For your business, if you filled up the employer contribution of the retirement plan, work with your financial professional to determine the maximum employee contribution for your circumstances. Fill up the bucket as a company employee, then move on to the next bucket. The IRS has a complicated formula to determine the amount you may contribute to a solo 401(k), SEP, or SIMPLE IRA. The IRS penalizes overages, so double-check by working with a tax professional.

4. DEDUCTIBLE CONTRIBUTIONS

Traditional IRA (Individual Retirement Account): If you can contribute to a traditional IRA, put in the maximum amount. This depends on your income level, whether or not you or your spouse has a workplace plan and your current age. Check out the IRS website for more details this year.

A traditional IRA is a wonderful savings vehicle, especially for those who think their retirement income levels will be *less* during retirement than now.

But this is a tricky question. Many people I ask this question automatically respond with, "Yes, of course, my retirement income will be less than I'm making now." Many of my clients who retire end up with a higher income during retirement. Mind blown, right? By the time you retire, you could be pulling in Social Security, a pension, rental properties, and other investment income totaling more than you're making now. Since we don't have a crystal ball, it's impossible to answer the question "to Roth or not to Roth" (see bucket #8 below). If you can contribute to a traditional IRA this year, you should do it. Contribute the maximum amount and move on to the next set of buckets.

Charitable contributions are a great way to accomplish two things at once. Reduce your taxable income and do some good in the world. Technically, you can contribute up to 50 percent of your income and have it deducted. I'm not advising you to fill this bucket before moving on to the next. However, if you are charitably inclined, consider being strategic about your philanthropic goals. Being a good steward of money means we have the privilege and responsibility of giving back to our communities. If this section applies to you, make a charitable plan every year. Here are some thoughts:

Not everything is tax deductible. According to the IRS, about 90 percent of Americans take the standard deduction. If you contribute to charitable organizations but take the standard deduction, the contribution won't lower your tax bracket. Be wary of those who tell you that "your generous contribution is tax deductible." It's not the case for most people.

If you want to ensure your contribution is tax-deductible, check out the organization's tax status. Some charities are not qualified 501(c)(3) organizations, so your gift won't be deductible. You can still contribute to them, but it will be with your after-tax dollars and won't lower your taxable income.

You can give other things besides cash (although cash is preferable for many charities). Consider your time, appreciated stock, vehicles, and other assets as donations.

One of my favorite ways to plan for charitable contributions and even pass a legacy down to your children or nieces or nephews is to establish something called a "DAF" or Donor Advised Fund. You can open up a DAF account at many brokerage firms. They usually require a $10,000 minimum contribution immediately deductible from your income if you itemize. The funds are in the account and invested through the company. You get to decide when and to whom the money goes. *Technically, you submit a request to the mutual fund company, and they must approve it. Before you open this type of account, make sure that you research the eligible recipients, fees, and other processes and procedures.

That's the end of the deferred and pre-tax savings buckets. Now we move on to money the IRS taxes, called taxable savings.

5. EMERGENCY FUNDS

Please put the oxygen mask on yourself first. If you do not have a fully funded emergency account, you are one bad month away from disaster. Referring to Chapter 2, we want to ensure that your family and your business have enough liquidity to sustain any emergency that comes your way. I suggest fully funding each of these emergency buckets and even getting an extra line of credit or credit card to use in case of emergency only.

Business savings should have two to three months of operating expenses. After your expense analysis, what is the minimum monthly amount needed to sustain your operations and pay all salaries? I'm only talking about the necessities here. Set this money aside in a savings account. Don't invest it. Don't spend it unless you absolutely need it – maybe because an earthquake rocked your office building, a recession is causing your customers to pull back, or your partner passed away. Now you need some extra liquidity before insurance pays out. Invest cash in excess of three months of savings. Fill this bucket up and move on to the next.

Personal savings should have two to 12 months of living expenses, depending on a few factors. Before COVID, the old sage advice was to have about three to six months of living expenses in your personal savings – enough to sustain you while you found a new job. I'm also talking about basic living expenses. (You will probably not go on luxury vacations if you lose your job.) You want to know how much it takes to feed and house your family for this time. The new savings advice depends on many factors: how close you are to retirement, your risk tolerance, your take on future inflation, and more. Again, don't invest this money, except maybe a short-term CD or other liquid types of instruments. You want to be able to access this money quickly if needed. Fill up the bucket, then move on to the kids.

6. CHILDREN'S SAVINGS

Saving for kids is a touchy subject. Many of my clients have children that they hope will attend college one day or are already attending college. Sometimes they feel guilty about filling up their retirement buckets when they haven't saved much for their kids' college tuition. Educating a child is a precious gift that we can bestow on the next generation. If we can do it without going into crippling debt (for you or the kid), it's even better.

You may be wondering if your kid will go to college. Perhaps you'd rather have your kid attend the school of hard knocks and learn through trial and error. You could instead put money into a down payment for their first home. You can save for a grand wedding or business startup. If you don't have biological or adopted children, then maybe you're the coolest auntie in the family, or you have fur babies instead.

Whatever the case, the textbook answer is to start saving early for the kids but not at the expense of your financial situation. The real-life answer is to artfully craft a balance of doing both simultaneously. Remember, life is not a textbook. Many options exist to help save for the kiddos. Below are a few ideas that are worth exploring with your financial professional. Some have tax benefits, and others do not. Whatever you decide, fill it up before moving on to the next bucket.

Examples of savings accounts for the kids or grandkids:

- 529 Accounts – State-sponsored college savings
- UGMA (Uniform Gift to Minors Act)/UTMA (Uniform Trust for Minors Act)
- Coverdell Accounts
- Taxable Savings

7. NON-DEDUCTIBLE CONTRIBUTIONS

We are now entering a world of excess. You've filled up all six other buckets with your hard-earned money and still have room for more savings. Congratulations, you are in the upper echelon of the Western world. You have more money to continue your savings journey. What do you do with it? Check the IRS website to see if you are eligible for the following after-tax retirement vehicles:

After-tax 401(k): Some employers allow after-tax contributions to company-sponsored retirement plans. You do have to pay taxes on the money now, but in the future, when you pull out the funds, you're only taxed on the gains from the investments. You can then do advanced strategies like Roth conversions with these after-tax 401(k) contributions. It's worth discussing this strategy with a financial professional.

Roth IRA: Your eligibility to contribute to a Roth IRA depends on your IRS taxable income. These are excellent vehicles for those who expect their retirement income to be lower than during their working years. You contribute anywhere from $6,500 to $7,500 annually, depending on your age and income. It's invested in whatever you wish (some can even get fancy by having a self-directed Roth IRA), and your only tax is on the gains when you pull out the money. As of this publication, capital gains tax brackets are usually lower than income tax brackets. Another advantage to Roth IRAs is the ability to take the money out before you turn 59½ years old due to education expenses, medical bills, first-time home buyers, and more. I recommend discussing this strategy with your tax professional.

8. TAXABLE SAVINGS

We are finally to the exciting stuff. Taxable savings are for those who have filled up all seven buckets, have their expenses and needs met, and still have cash left over. If this sounds like your situation, this is where you can have fun. I'm not talking about going to Las Vegas and gambling all your money away, but I am talking about the ability to take on a little bit more risk to increase your net worth. The IRS has already taxed this bucket of savings. You save money here and invest it for the future. Once you sell those investments, you are taxed on the capital gain. For example, if you bought a duplex with the savings in this bucket for $300,000, then sold it ten years later for $375,000, your only tax is the capital gains of $75,000. Whatever you decide to invest in with this money, make sure that it's appropriate for your risk profile. See Chapter 11 for how to craft your own investment policy statement.

Case Study: The Successful Consultant

Meet Khrissy: Khrissy is the type who doesn't take "no" for an answer. She built up a successful consulting practice that spans four states, five employees, and a dozen consultants. She had previously brought on a few partners but decided that it needed to be easier to steer the ship, so she bought them out. Khrissy did all of this while raising three children independently and working as a consultant for several large clients.

Khrissy's Goals: From yesterday, Khrissy wants to retire in three and a half years. She has a book she has been writing and wants to finish it after she retires. She owns real estate in multiple states and wants to teach her oldest child how to manage her properties so she can eventually go into real estate independently. Khrissy is an avid traveler and doesn't plan to stop her jet-set life after retirement. She thinks that she has a good financial plan, but she wants a professional set of eyes to look at her plan.

Khrissy's Obstacles: She has some significant health problems that have precluded her from getting reasonably priced insurance. Khrissy doesn't have plans to date or get married ever again, so long-term care will be a point of discussion in her family. She has an extremely high income, which means tax mitigation is crucial. Khrissy's real estate investments are also causing her cash flow issues and high debt. However, it's imperative to Khrissy that she can maintain her lifestyle rather than be beholden to a budget.

Khrissy's Outcome: Khrissy's life was in an Excel spreadsheet. She built a spreadsheet she had used for ten years, maybe longer. To her, the spreadsheet looked great. I pointed out that her spreadsheet did not account for factors like inflation, bear markets, disability, and more. The Excel spreadsheet needed updating, and many formulas needed corrections. We took her Excel document and put it into financial planning software. When I initially showed her the financial plan as she had it written, the software showed a dismal ten percent chance of success in meeting her goals. She simply had not been saving all these years, and her savings were not the maximum. Khrissy was spending money like there was no tomorrow, even though she hoped for a different type of tomorrow.

We identified many problems in her plan that stemmed back to the almighty cash flow discussion. Khrissy and her family were overspending, even though she was a highly successful consultant and real estate guru. She was overpaying in taxes and needed to save more for her retirement. Khrissy needed mitigation plans and important estate planning documents in place.

We ran scenarios that included high inflation, disability, and bear markets. Through our relationship, we could not only get her financial affairs in order but also identify her habits and underlying mindset about her finances. Today, she is training her replacement in the company and looking forward to the day her junior consultant will buy her out. Unfortunately, she can't retire in a couple of years, but her plan forward is clear now. Khrissy has fixed her cash flow issues, and her plan now boasts a 100 percent chance of success if she stays the course.

Chapter 6

The 5 Ds: Mitigating Risk

Financial planning is the process of looking at your current assets and comparing them to your future goals. We then find a way to reach your goals with what you have now. Think of financial planning like a bridge. We are building a bridge to get to your goals. On one side of the bridge are your assets and liabilities now. On the other side of the bridge are your future plans, like retirement, buying a vacation home, sending the kids to college, or living to the end of your life without burdening your children. Each wooden plank of the bridge is a financial planning strategy that gets you closer to your goals.

Some techniques that might help you include...

- Saving more
- Spending less
- Investing in the stock market
- Insurance
- Selling a business
- Real estate
- Dividends or recurring income
- Compounding interest
- ...and more!

Risk is not a bad thing. You took an enormous risk by starting your own business and leaving your cushy job in the corporate world. However, if you have yet to account for something called *risk*, your wooden bridge could one day come crashing down, leaving you short of your goals. You may have felt burnt out and stressed, but you received regular and reliable income supporting your lifestyle. Did the reward of leaving your job and starting a business outweigh the risk of doing so? I hope the answer is yes. You took on the risk because you saw a need or untapped market, and the upside was more significant than the downside. Hopefully, you've thought through any other risks of owning a business.

If you don't have plans to mitigate some of this risk, your hopes and dreams could come crashing down in a single instant. You would never reach your short, mid, or long-term goals. Your family may suffer. You may suffer. The ending of that story could be a lot better.

"The 5 Ds," coined by the Exit Planning Institute in Ohio, says everyone will experience at least one of these 5 risks in our lifetime. Can you guess which one? How will you mitigate any of these risk factors going forward?

 Head over to www.growthconsultingfirm.com/resources to grab your 5 D's Worksheet.

The 5 Ds (i.e., Risk that could potentially wipe out your hard work)

Death

- Your death
- Your spouse's death
- An elderly family member's death
- Your business partner's death
- Your key employee's death

Disability

- You can't work for a few months because of chemo treatments
- You can't work at your job function because of a car accident
- Your spouse becomes disabled and can't work
- Your child becomes disabled and requires care
- Your key employee becomes disabled and can no longer support your business

Disagreement

- You have a disagreement with your business partner
- You have a disagreement with your key employee
- You have a disagreement with a major client

Divorce

- What happens to your children?
- Who gets the house?
- Who gets the dog?
- What happens to your business?
- What happens to you?

Disaster

- There's another lockdown like COVID
- We go through a recession
- There's an earthquake, and your building becomes condemned
- There's a fire or flood
- What's the contingency plan for your employees, your family, your clients?

As you can see, we can dream up countless "what-if" scenarios. Because the future is so uncertain, many of these scenarios can repeatedly play in our heads while lying in bed trying to sleep. The stress of the unknown can cause anxiety that spills over into other parts of our lives. Although we can't ever be certain of the future, there are steps we can take to lessen the potentially devastating impact of the unknown. These steps will only partially protect you, but they can help you continue your financial plan without complete ruin. My clients lovingly call this my "Doom and Gloom" discussion.

This chapter can be painful to read, but rest assured I have a solution for you. Head to https://www.growthconsultingfirm.com/resources to grab your "5 Ds" worksheet.

Your situation is unique and unlike anyone else on this planet. I've listed some possible solutions to mitigate the risk of each of the 5 Ds. However, not all solutions will apply to your situation. Make sure that you discuss these with a professional.

Potential Tools to Soften the Blows from the 5 Ds: i.e., Ways to Mitigate Risk

Death

Tools: Insurance Plan/Continuity Plan/Emergency Savings/Important Documents

- Your death – Do you have appropriate insurance covering your earnings and debts?

- Your spouse's death – Do you have an updated last will and testament or a revocable trust?

- An elderly family member's death – How much is in your emergency savings?

- Your business partner's death – What is the continuity plan? Do you have buy/sell insurance?

- Your key employee's death – Are your operating manuals in order to transfer knowledge within your company?

Disability

Medical Power of Attorney/Income Replacement/Emergency Savings

- You can't work for a few months because of chemo treatments. Can you use your emergency savings to pay for living expenses while you're out of work?

- You can't work at your job function because of a car accident. What type of income replacement do you have?

- Your spouse becomes disabled and can't work. Do you have adequate disability insurance?

- Your child becomes disabled and requires care. Have discussions now with your spouse or partner, even if you're speaking about hypotheticals.

- Your key employee becomes disabled and can no longer support your business. Ensure that everyone at your company (even you) is easily replaceable.

Disagreement

Buy-Sell Agreements/Insurance/Contracts: Employee, Vendors, Stakeholders

- You have a disagreement with your business partner. Do stakeholders know of a continuity plan if you go your separate ways?

- You have a disagreement with your key employee. What type of key man insurance is in place?

- You have a disagreement with a major client. Ensure that you have well-written contracts.

Divorce

Proper Asset Titling/Guardianship of Children & Pets/Income Replacement

- What happens to your children? Guardianship plans can ease the transition for children.

- Who gets the house? Ensure that all your assets have proper titles.

- What happens to your business? Trusts can be effective instruments in ensuring your business has protection from your ex-spouse or even your child's ex-spouse. Talk to a lawyer.

- What happens to you? Financial freedom means that you have income that is independent of another power.

Disaster

Continuity Plan: Go-bag, Meeting Location, Evacuation, Next of Kin /Emergency Savings/Insurance Review

- There's another lockdown like COVID. Do you have access to quick capital?

- We go through a recession. How often do you forecast and plan?

- There's an earthquake, and your building is condemned. Review your insurance needs at least annually.

- There's a fire or flood. Communicate your continuity plan to all stakeholders and consider even initiating a call tree.

What's the contingency plan for your employees, your family, your clients?

As you can see, there are things you can do to mitigate the risk and after-shock of any of these 5 Ds. We never know what will happen or the severity of such events. However, by planning for these risks, we can lessen the overall impact and decrease the toll it will take. Planning for these will also help you worry less because you know you did everything within your control.

When my father passed in 2022, my brothers and I had a difficult time deciding next steps. We were overwhelmed by grief and couldn't think straight. My dad didn't have a valid will in place; his wishes had only been communicated verbally throughout the years. Fortunately, our spouses had the wherewithal to guide us during the time – to tell us to eat, to clean, to make important decisions and so on. I truly believe that a valid Last Will and Testament is a beautiful gift to leave to your beneficiaries. Take it from me!

Below is the most crucial section of the entire book. Work with your estate planning attorney and make sure that, at a minimum, you have an updated and valid Last Will and Testament, Powers of Attorney, and more. Your loved ones will thank you for the preparation you've done.

Read your last will and testament if it's over five years old.

Also, ensure your loved ones know where to locate these items. If you have unmarried adult children, you may also want to talk to them about their documents.

Last Will & Testament or Trust	Ensure your wishes are laid out
Medical Power of Attorney	Who can make decisions for you if you become incapacitated?
Durable Power of Attorney	If you cannot act for yourself, who do you trust to act for you?
Guardianship Designation	If you have minor children or are thinking about having children
Letter of Intent	Write to your beneficiaries or executor of your estate
Beneficiary Updates	Review your account beneficiaries, especially after a major life event

A note about insurance: An insurance product can be very beneficial to people. However, insurance is only one of the planks we can use to build the bridge that gets us closer to our goals. Too often, I see clients who have patched together insurance policies over the years. They might have term insurance + whole life + umbrella + and more. An approach that once served a particular purpose is no longer serving their life because things have drastically changed, yet they are still paying the premiums.

I urge you to review your policies, specifically the death benefits, the coverage, waiting periods, the premiums, and the beneficiaries. Does it all still work for your current life? If not, consider getting an unbiased opinion from a fee-only financial planner who doesn't earn commissions on life insurance or other products. An independent insurance agent can often give you a very unbiased look at your policies. They can tell you objectively whether you need more insurance or have the proper insurance already in place.

A note about buy-sell agreements: If you have key employees or partners, ensuring that your buy-sell agreements are watertight and reflect your company's most up-to-date version is essential. Sometimes owners write up a quick contract when they first start the business. Fast forward 20+ years, and one owner dies, leaving a hole in the business and a massive liability for the other partner. Or a divorce of another partner causes new ownership in the business that was unexpected and unwanted. Make a point to review your buy-sell agreements regularly to decrease the risk to your business and personal life.

Case Study: Story of the Widow

Meet Mary: I'll never forget the day I met Mary. Her husband had passed away, and she had no idea what to do with her finances. With the gentle nudging of her daughter, she reluctantly made an appointment to come into our office. Her nails were red, swollen, and bitten down as far as she could. I will always remember her fingernails. She wept in the conference room and told me how her husband had taken care of everything, and she didn't even know how to pay her utility bills. She was in her early 60s and had never learned how to do anything "financial," as she put it. She dutifully cared for her children and had a robust career for decades, but she couldn't understand a financial statement well enough to know what to do about it.

Mary's Goals: She wanted to find an advisor she could trust. She wanted to discover a path forward that included education, a listening ear, and potential happiness as a widow.

Mary's Obstacles: Mary's husband distrusted financial advisors and had clear investment convictions. Mary tried to do things his way but didn't always agree with his philosophies.

Mary's Outcomes: I took her financial statements and broke them down in plain English throughout the following year. I worked with her bill by bill until she had a firm grasp on budgeting. We looked at her new income flows, insurance benefits, and healthcare. We worked to find the investment convictions and goals she had and wanted to pursue while still paying tribute to her late husband.

After a few months, her fingernails turned pink. I could see a spark of life back in her eyes. Her daughter even took her to get a manicure. One day, she walked into the office with a little more pep and told me that she was ready to set some goals. She wanted to begin planning for the future. It wasn't her expected future, but it looked brighter every day. Mary had regained her confidence, and we built a financial plan for her that would leave a legacy to her children, grandchildren, and favorite charities.

Unfortunately, I've encountered many widows and divorcees and helped them through grieving. It's messy. It's sad. It can take a long time. They say, "an ounce of prevention is worth a pound of cure." My goal with my business is to ensure that women don't have this extra layer of stress when they end up alone later in life. No woman should have to feel vulnerable and afraid about her finances. Together, let's change the way we talk about money.

Section II:
Learn to Scale Your Business

Chapter 7

Debt & Capital Expenditures

"Never borrow money on something that depreciates."
— **William Cleland**

Not all debt is bad. Debt can be a wise tool to create leverage and grow a company to the next level. This chapter discusses Good vs. Evil debt. The rule of thumb is to follow the ROI (return on investment) when using debt. Because debt is not free, you want to make sure that any debt you take on will give you a higher return than what you are paying. William Cleland recommends borrowing money only on an asset that increases in value. Think of a personal vehicle in this example. If you purchase a shiny new car, the value decreases when you drive it out of the dealer's lot. You could not turn around and sell it to someone else for the same amount you purchased it for, let alone more than what you bought it for. If you borrowed money to purchase this shiny new car, your return on investment is negative. The lesson is to use cash or debt without an interest fee if buying a car.

On the flip side of this equation is the possibility of using debt on an asset that increases with value beyond what you use to pay for the debt. You can use your business to leverage up. For example, getting a mortgage to buy a rental property that gives you positive cash flow and grows in value over time is a smart way to use debt. Apply this principle to your business and the daily business decisions you must make.

Let's discuss two types of debt: secured and unsecured debt. Collateral, an asset equal to the money you owe, backs secured debt. Because a bank can repossess the asset if you fail to repay your loan, the rates tend to be lower than an unsecured loan, for example. That's not always the case, however. I urge you to talk to your local banker before you need a loan. The landscape constantly changes, and banks are constantly evolving their debt products and offerings. Don't assume you know what's out there. Shop around *before* you get into a situation where you desperately need a loan. Remember, it's always easier to get credit when times are good. It's more difficult to get credit when times are lean.

Unsecured debt does not have any specific asset that the bank can repossess. Think about a credit card. You could use the credit card to buy whatever you want. If you fail to pay back to the bank, they can't come and repossess your purse, fancy restaurant meal, or shoes. Because of this lack of collateral, the rates tend to be higher. Again, there are exceptions, such as student loans. Student loans have lower loan rates, but the bank can't come and repossess your brain or college degree, thankfully!

	Secured Debt		Unsecured Debt
☑	Collateral used to secure the debt	☑	No collateral is used to secure the debt
☑	Rates tend to be lower	☑	Rates tend to be higher
☑	Used for real estate, vehicles, equipment	☑	Used for credit cards, personal loans, student loans

Why we use debt

- To live beyond our means; we can't pay cash, so we put it on credit
- To Improve our situation as we work toward a goal
- As leverage to get an even higher rate of return

Let's assume you want to get a loan to leverage your current assets and achieve a higher ROI. How much debt should you take on?

Credit Cards and Unsecured Loans to fund our lifestyles and emergencies

- Avoid or pay off the entire balance every month

- Access to credit cards and unsecured loans can be an alternative way to fund cash needs in the case of emergencies or unexpected opportunities for growth

- Be wary of high interest rates

House: a mortgage to pay for our home over time

- Rule of thumb = (monthly home costs/monthly gross income) < 28 percent

- Don't buy more home than you can afford. If you add up your monthly mortgage, insurance, taxes, and maintenance, divide that by your total monthly gross income. Your answer should be less than 28 percent. In other words, less than 28 percent of your income should go toward your house. Don't be "house poor" and remain confined to your home. You still want to go on vacations, go out to dinner with friends, and other activities.

Education: student loans give us access to knowledge and networks

- Your post-graduation monthly loan payment should be 10 percent or less of your take-home pay in your new career.

- The gift of a debt-free education is one precious gift that we can give to our children. When they graduate from college or technical school, or any other type of education, the last thing they need is a crushing pile of debt on their shoulders. There is a way to let your child have a vested interest in their education, pay for part or all of it themselves, get scholarships, or start saving from the time they are born. Make it a win-win for everyone.

Business: use debt as leverage to achieve even higher results

- Start or expand a business that will ultimately have a high rate of return.

- Take out a short-term loan to buy or lease equipment that will allow your company to grow.

- Use debt to hire an employee that will quickly grow your revenue or bring in new clients.

- Purchase a building for your office and lease out the remaining units to pay the rent.

That's how you use debt to grow your business! Refrain from using debt in your business to buy a T-shirt or a new printer. Those things depreciate, and you probably should only purchase them if you have enough cash to buy them outright.

How to pay down "bad" debt

Some of you have "bad" debt from your previous life. Let's plan to pay off that bad debt as soon as possible. Not only is it preventing you from living your fullest life, but owing money to someone is a chip we will take off your shoulders starting today.

 Head over to www.growthconsultingfirm.com/resources to get your blank template on How to Pay Down "Bad" Debt.

Here's a step-by-step process to getting out of debt and living your best life.

1. Take inventory of all your liabilities (total outstanding amount, interest rate, monthly payment)

Institution Name	Name(s) on the Account	Total Outstanding Balance	Interest Rate	Minimum Monthly Payment
Example: Credit union	Husband and wife joint	$10,000	7.99%	$205
Example: big bank	Wife only	$4,500	15.99%	$199

2. Put all of your liabilities on **autopay** to pay the minimum monthly amount. Include these amounts in your monthly household or business budget.

3. Set a non-monetary "Reward" for paying off each account. For example, will you do a happy dance? Open that bottle of wine that you've been saving? Take a long bubble bath?

Institution Name	Name(s) on the Account	Total Outstanding Balance	Interest Rate	Minimum Monthly Payment	Reward
Example: Credit union	Husband and wife joint	$10,000	7.99%	$205	Open the bottle of wine that we have been saving!
Example: big bank	Wife only	$4,500	15.99%	$199	Massage at the Nordic Spa

4. Identify your most expensive debt (highest interest rate). Decide how much room you have in your budget to pay extra on this account.

5. Pay your highest interest rate account first until you have paid it off completely and there is a zero balance.

Priority	Institution Name	Name(s) on the Account	Total Outstanding Balance	Interest Rate	Min. Monthly Payment	Extra Monthly Payment	Reward
2	Example: Credit union	Husband and wife joint	$8,000	7.99%	$205	$0	Open the bottle of wine that we have been saving!
1	Example: Big bank	Wife only	$14,500	15.99%	$199	$650	Massage at the Nordic Spa

6. Collect your "Reward" for paying off this account.

7. Repeat steps 4 through 6 with the remaining accounts.

You might need more immediate satisfaction. Instant gratification is very satisfying. If you are the type that needs to play mind tricks on yourself, pay off the lowest balance first instead of the lowest interest rate first. This strategy will allow you to get a taste of freedom from debt. When you pay off your first balance, you'll get a rush of happy endorphins and want to pay off even more debt. Sometimes paying off the highest interest rate balance means waiting months or even years. You know yourself better than anyone. Stick to the strategy that works best for you.

Chapter 8

Expense Analysis: Scale Wisely

Each year, CEOs and executives conduct an in-depth expense audit of all their departments, projects, personnel, travel, operating, and more. The CEO needs to have a clear understanding of what it takes to run the business right now and into the future. You are creating a money-making machine with your business.

Money In - Money Out = Profit

Even though you are accomplishing great things through your business, at the end of the day, your business is just a vehicle to achieve your mission. You could have chosen any business, but your mission, vision, and values are the same. When I was back in my corporate days, it always seemed as if someone was asking us to do more with fewer resources. It can be very frustrating, but it can also be a way to force a business owner to be more innovative with their current resources.

As a business owner, you should do a complete "expense audit" annually. From there, you can build your budget for the year. "Lifestyle creep" is a term used to describe how increased income gradually leads to increased spending over time. We go out to eat more often because we bring home more money. We look at luxury cars instead of new, used cars. We shop more often because we "think" we can afford it. I call this exercise "financial burpees". This activity is a high-intensity exercise that doesn't take too long to complete but yields great results. No one likes this exercise, but it is very good for your fiscal health. An expense audit is essential, so make sure to complete this chapter.

First, let's talk about the B-word: your budget. What do you think of when I say budget? What images or experiences come up for you? Many of my clients think of diets and restrictions. They think of going without, going hungry, or sacrificing. I want to offer another viewpoint that may empower you to think about a budget differently. When you stick to a budget, you're not depriving yourself of anything. A budget gives you more *power* to do more in this world. You've probably heard the saying, "money makes the world go 'round." It's true.

When you spend your money, you put your influence into the world.

Think of it: You decide where you spend your money, on a vacation, a subscription, clothing, dinner, a new bicycle, or tuition for your kids. You are the one deciding where that money is going, and that money then cranks the engine of the business on the receiving end. Right? If you follow a budget for your business (or personal life), you potentially have leftover money that you can use at your discretion. We call that a discretionary budget.

The surplus that remains becomes your power and influence on your community. Will you spend it supporting that local small business you love? Will you binge-shop on Amazon after a hard day's work? Will you buy that expensive car to drive around town? Will you infuse some capital into a nonprofit in your neighborhood? Will you save it to build the future you've always dreamed of? If you think about it this way, it could change how you feel about your money. Remember this power theme as you go through your burpees.

As always, remember that I am right here with you so that you don't have to do your "burpees" alone. From one boss lady to another, you can do this!

 Head over to https://www.growthconsultingfirm.com/resources and download your Expense Analysis Excel worksheet.

Step 1: Download the last 12 calendar months of expenses into a spreadsheet.

You either do this bank account by account or fuse them into one spreadsheet. The organization depends on how many "departments" you may have. Next, go through the spreadsheet with a fine-tooth comb and categorize these expenses into one of three buckets.

A. Needed (Green)

How much do you need to keep the lights on? What expenses are for your licenses, professional fees, taxes, inventory, and other necessities? These charges are the bare minimum expenses you need to keep your business up and running. These are all the items you need; without them, you could force the closure of your doors.

B. Nice to Have (Yellow)

We want to see the difference between what is essential in your business and what is the fluff that makes you more comfortable. What do you spend your money on that is nice but unnecessary?

C. Not Needed (Red)

These expenses are not necessary in your business and have sucked up your dollars for little or no return on investment. Remember that as an entrepreneur, you are looking for a healthy return on investment on every single penny. Expenses are an investment into your business, without which you cannot function. That means that if an expense has crept into your annual spending, it's time to identify it, then kill it. Some examples are subscriptions to fancy software you never use and an administrative person doing more personal errands than business work for you.

One of my clients paid expensive rent for an office she never used. We eliminated this expense immediately and overnight increased her profitability. All her clients were virtual, but she felt she wasn't a valid business if she didn't have a physical office with her company's name. Once she got over her imposter syndrome of having to be in a physical office, she was able to increase her profitability and use the excess cash for other investments into her business.

Step 2: Build your budget for the next 12 months

Building a budget is an extremely important step in the operation of your business. The 12-month budget is useful for all kinds of decisions, through thick and thin. It keeps a company on track during the course of the year if aligned to the owner's goals and vision.

1. Return to your "Needed" expenses and begin categorizing even further. These categories should match your profit & loss categories of expenses. Add up the total for each category, which becomes your operating budget. In the accounting world, it's called the chart of accounts. Here's an example.

Expenses

Google	$12	12 months
Canva	$12	12 months
Calendly	$35	12 months
Phone line	$20	12 months
Certification annual renewal	$300	
Virtual Assistant	$700	12 months
Lease – Excavation Equipment	$1400	12 months
Lease – Truck	$900	12 months
Lease – Office Rent	$2100	12 Months

Chart of Accounts and Corresponding Budget Totals

2023 Software Budget	$720
2023 Labor	$8,400
2023 Dues & Certification	$300
2023 Lease Equipment	$27,600
2023 Lease Office	$25,200
2023 Needed Expenses	**$87,420**

2. Now repeat the above process for your "Nice to Have" expenses. For example:

Social media manager	$750	12 months
Client gifts	$30	22 items
Coffee meetings	$11	24 meetings
Company mugs	$150	
Company pens	$120	
Annual conference out of state	$650	
2023 Social Media	$9,000	
2023 Travel Budget	$650	
2023 Client gifts	$660	
2023 Company Swag	$270	
2023 Coffee Meetings	$264	
2023 Total Nice to Have:	**10,844**	

3. Eliminate unwanted and unnecessary expenses as soon as humanly possible. Cancel the subscriptions and commit to using restraint when spending. We will use these dollars for other more important revenue-generating tasks in the coming year. Still, go ahead and add this all up for the year. How much did you spend on unwanted items?

Magazine Ad	$1,200
Software A	$1,000
Software B	$2,890
Upwork Contract	$4,015
Total Unneeded Expenses 2022	**$9,105**

Now we will find out how much this number will help you in the coming year. As the CEO and president of your company, you can formally announce how much you saved this year by cutting costs and adopting a leaner operating budget!

Total Unneeded Expenses Last 12 months x 100 = % Saved!
(Total all expenses)

$$\frac{\$9,105 \times 100}{\$107,369} = \textbf{8.5\% saved!}$$

Give yourself a giant pat on the back! Send yourself a digital congratulatory card. Smile for 30 seconds. Well done, boss lady! You are such a wise and efficient leader.

If you get rid of the "Nice to Haves" as well, you become even more efficient!

$$\frac{(\$9,105 + \$10,844)}{\$107,369} \times 100 = \textbf{18.5\% saved!}$$

The needed expenses are your budget for the next fiscal year. Keep these 2023 numbers readily available because you'll use them for forecasting later.

4. Put a reminder on your calendar to do a budget analysis once a year. Stop right now and enter this reminder.

Step 3: Start an emergency savings for your operating expenses

What is your slowest revenue season? How many months does it last? For me, the summer is usually the slowest. Clients are on vacation, and many are thinking about spending their hard-earned money, not saving it. In Alaska especially, I joke that my clients disappear for three months, occasionally popping in to say hi when they need something, then running away again. They're busy fishing, camping, traveling out of state, and making the most of their summer daylight. That's OK for me because I'm doing the same thing, and I anticipated this slowdown in revenue.

Your minimum emergency savings amount is your needed expenses multiplied by the number of months in your slow season. For this example, your emergency savings could be $45,000 x 3 = $135,000. This amount is the minimum amount of cash you need to survive if you have zero clients or revenue.

Your maximum emergency savings amount is your needed expenses plus your discretionary spending. (Needed expenses + Nice to Have expenses) x number of slow months. For this example, it could be ($45,000 + $15,000) x 3 = $180,000, the maximum amount of cash equivalent you want on hand.

Companies may only need two months of expenses in their emergency savings account. Sometimes having too much cash can be a deterrent to your growth. Extra cash might be better suited to earning a return in your company through hiring an extra set of hands, a new product rollout, or a piece of operating equipment. Using the example above, if I only needed two months of expenses in my emergency savings account, I would con-sider a range of $90,000 ($45,000 x 2 months) to $120,000 ($60,000 x 2).

An emergency savings account for the business is so vital for your liquidity. Remember Chapter 2. Can you pay your bills? Many small companies ceased operation in 2020 because they couldn't pay their bills during the lockdown. If you have enough cash to withstand a lockdown, you have essentially bought yourself time to think of a way to pivot your business, survive an economic turndown, and not worry about revenue for a short period. At the bare minimum, you must have your needed expenses covered worry-free. You can always cut your nice-to-have expenses while you tighten your belt for a while. Your company can run on the bare minimum. What it can't do is run for a long time on gas fumes, negative cash or borrowing cash to survive.

Accounts Payable

The money you owe your vendors for their services or products is accounts payable. A note about vendors: Remember your vendors are a business just like you and maybe even a small business like you. They depend on your payment as their revenue stream, just as you rely on your customers for your revenue stream. Please pay your colleague on time, every time. Doing so is just a business courtesy for those with good manners. However, for your cash flow reasons, I highly encourage you to **get paid fast but pay slowly.**

How slowly can you pay your vendors while still maintaining a great relationship? Can you pay them in installments over time (without added interest)? Can you break up your payments into two or three installments? Can you pay on the back end after the service is complete? Many small business owners can negotiate terms. When you pay slowly, you are freeing up your cash flow. Remember that money owed increases your liability as accounts payable on your balance sheet. In other words, your debt balance goes up. You are fine if you still have the cash to cover this future obligation.

A client told me they pride themselves on paying their vendors as quickly as possible. Sam Walton, the founder of Walmart, is known to give this advice. This client wants to take care of their vendors because it is a part of their culture of excellence. They pay faster than any of their competitors, and they know that they have the upper hand in negotiation. "Get paid fast but pay slowly" is more of an art than an exact science. You know your vendors and competitors best. Ensure that you have a handle on this concept. You'll want to take care of your partners and reputation, but never at the expense of your cash flow.

Additional Note about Accounts Payable: Don't forget to include other payables that come up during the course of business. For example, taxes owed on the revenue you collect are Accounts Payable to the IRS. Also, if you have a sales team that works on commissions, the amount that you owe to them also becomes an Account Payable. Some owners get into hot water because they forget about setting this revenue aside. The money is not yours, so don't spend it on anything other than taxes or commissions.

Accounts Receivable

Money your clients owe you is accounts receivable. I suggest getting your payment as soon as possible. Apple, Inc. averages less than 30 days DSO (Days Sales Outstanding). In September 2022, their average days to collect payments from their customers was 18.5 days, according to their shareholder report. Any company or customer that does business with Apple must pay them within 18.5 days. I've seen clients with over 365 days to get payment for services rendered. Don't let that be you. You depend on this cash to survive, make payroll, and invest in your future. Forty-five days should be the maximum to get paid, which is still on the long side of the deal. Make sure you tell your customers in advance of signing any contract or receiving any product. Lay out expectations about payment structure initially. Doing so is also excellent customer service as you lay the groundwork for your relationship with your client. Your wallet will thank you, and your client will appreciate the professionalism.

Run your DSO report monthly. If you see any accounts receivable on the list older than 45 days, plan to begin calling on this account as soon as possible. Sometimes calling someone else in the company is a simple yet powerful strategy for collecting payment. Remember to be nice. The bill might be overdue because someone misplaced it, the company had a recent turnover, or they are in financial distress. You want to preserve this relationship. However, I advise discontinuing work with this client if the overdue bill remains unpaid after a few months. As the boss lady, you get to decide what the parameters are for this policy.

Case Study: Meet the Nonprofit Executive Director

Meet the Nonprofit: A Florida organization run by a charismatic executive director quadrupled the organization's income in less than two years. The organization, deeply embedded in the community, does wonderful things for its clients and stakeholders. The organization has one full-time employee and several outstanding interns from the local university. The Board of Directors are new but eager to help.

The Nonprofit's Goals: To increase its footprint in the state and come out of the pandemic flourishing and thriving by supporting other local nonprofits and community members.

The Nonprofit's Obstacles: An inexperienced Board of Directors and a global pandemic that inhibits communication and makes finding the people it supports difficult.

The Nonprofit's Outcome: The Board asked for financial statements and reporting for several months. However, the executive director always said the financials were "good" and would communicate with us as needed. Unfortunately, we found out from the only full-time employee that the funds disappeared. The ED had failed to meet payroll, spent the funds, and had a zero account balance. The Board immediately called for his resignation. We later found through an investigation that he did not commit fraud but had misused appropriated funds.

I served as the organization's interim crisis CFO, going from over $1,000,000 in receipts to $0 overnight. We had to close the organization and hand off the mission to local groups who could take on more caseloads. The nonprofit failed to manage its budget and cash flow wisely. Even though we were promised grants and donations to our organization, the ED couldn't keep the lights on at the end of the day.

All members of nonprofit boards, business owners, and stakeholders should always know what to ask for regarding financials, when to ask for it, and what it all means. Fortunately for you reading this book, you now have a toolbox full of resources to look into your or another's financials. You can see how financial acumen is critically essential for any business owner or leader.

Chapter 9

Labor: Operating the Machine

Have you ever read the "Fortune 500 Fastest Growing Companies" magazine issue? It's inspiring to see all the great company founders on the glossy pages, reading about their successes and stories. The Kauffman Foundation and Inc Magazine conducted a study on these Fortune 500 Fastest Growing companies. They wanted to know where the founders and the companies were in business five to eight years after appearing in the magazine. What they found was astonishing and disheartening. Many companies were either sold at a disadvantage, back to square one, or bankrupt. While the research report doesn't cite the exact reasoning behind this, we can make an educated guess. Experts at the Growth Institute[8] believe these companies hired too quickly or incorrectly. I think many founders tried to grow their companies with the same mindset they had when they started the business. Mix in optimism and cash flow beyond their wildest dreams and experience, and you have a recipe for disaster. As the saying goes:

Cash Is King and if you don't have a grip on your cash, then you don't have a king.

Because your company is growing, you know you need more hands and brains to run the business now. You alone are not enough to sustain this machine you built. Our days have only 24 hours built into them. It's

---

[8] https://blog.growthinstitute.com/scale-up-blueprint/10-mistakes-startups-make-under-rapid-growth

impossible to run your business with only one person now. You must hire wisely to further your mission and ensure the machine doesn't collapse. Here are some fundamental labor and hiring areas to focus on when growing your company. Manage these wisely, and you'll make it to the end. Congratulations on getting to this point in your company's lifecycle!

Owner Work and Compensation

When consulting with women business owners, I see three themes regarding owner pay. Some of these owners pay themselves a regular and reasonable salary. But many of these owners either don't pay themselves a living wage or they take whatever the leftovers in the bank account at the end of the month as their pay; sometimes it's a lot, sometimes it's not very much at all.

Let's talk about what the IRS wants to see. It's important to set up your legal structure from the beginning. The salaries and wages paid should fit into your legal structure. If you are a sole proprietor or LLC, the revenue flows through the business anyway, so it doesn't matter to the IRS what you pay yourself.

The IRS will look for a reasonable salary if your business structure is an S-corporation. There are a lot of tests they employ to determine what your reasonable salary should be. Ensure you work with a trusted tax advisor to determine what this number is for your business.

One test the IRS will use is the reasonable salary test.[9] Affectionately I call it the "hat test." Think about all the hats you wear in the business. What tasks do you do daily? Are you the head of HR, marketing, customer

---

[9] https://www.irs.gov/businesses/small-businesses-self-employed/paying-yourself

service, and construction staff? Do you make the products and deliver them to your customers? Do you file payroll and make sales calls?

If you had to hire someone to replace you, how many people would you hire, and what would you pay those people?

Add up all these hats, and that amount might be your reasonable salary.

The IRS will also test your prior experience and what other people doing the same duties pay themselves. If you choose the S-corp election on your tax forms or a C-corporation, you will save on taxes because the company will then begin paying for your FICA taxes, but it also opens you up to an increased chance of an audit. It's OK to be audited! Audits are not bad, as many people may lead you to think. The IRS is trying to find individuals getting meager salaries from their businesses but taking large distributions unnecessarily. Why is this important? Because the IRS taxes wages at the income tax bracket level; owner distributions are capital gains, usually lower than the income tax brackets. Don't be that person who tries to cheat their way out of taxes.

Your business should be paying you a reasonable salary plus maybe an additional premium for taking on the risk of being a business owner. If you aren't getting paid enough by your own company, then why don't you just go get a job? Employees don't carry the same risk or stress of running a company.

Growing the Team

You must consider many different factors when you hire an employee. In this section, we'll talk about just a few of the considerations from a financial perspective.

Right now, head to www.growthconsultingfirm.com/resources to grab your worksheet for "Growing the Team." Then come back here and follow along.

Step 1: Write down every task you do personally.

Now that you are growing, you have the wonderful privilege of hiring people to help you. Your time is precious, and you should use it to grow the business, not complete tasks you could outsource for a lesser hourly rate. I often hear about owners cleaning toilets, doing the bookkeeping, and putting together sales proposals. It's time to take inventory of all your daily tasks. Track your actions for a month in a notebook or online document. Look at your list and note all the jobs you don't like to do.

Find someone to take over these tasks as soon as possible. Outline the remaining tasks into an organizational chart for the business. We are trying to save your sanity, plus a new owner will one day come in and want to replace you. Of course, there is only one YOU, but if you are doing eight different jobs for the price of one, it's going to be challenging to sell your business. In the end, we are selling your business to a new owner.

My tasks as an owner

Social Media Posts

Taking out the trash

Payroll

Invoicing Clients

Updating the CRM

Onboarding Clients

Preparing Client Meetings

Client Portfolios

Paying Bills

Answering the phone

Scheduling appointments

Creating a brochure

Updating the Website

Following up with vendors

Reviewing Financials

Meet with the CPA

Sending Client Cards

Compliance

Renewing Licenses

Trade Shows

Conferences

Continuing Education ...and more

Step 2: Build your ideal organizational chart

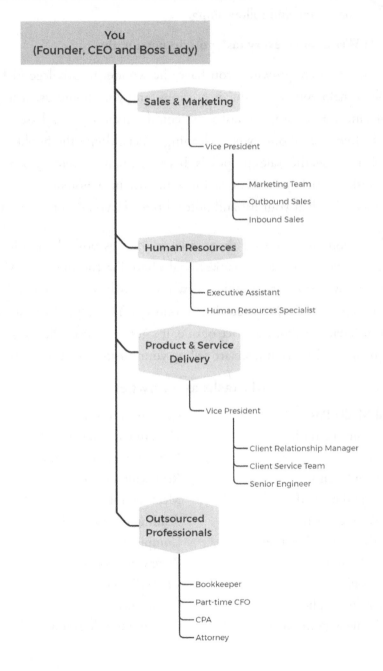

You are the CEO/founder at the top. You may have a cofounder. Who else do you need to help complete the tasks on your list? Balance your idealism with reality. You may want to hire an entire sales team ultimately, but it would be great if you had a sales assistant for now. Think of the next 12 to 24 months when you build this chart out.

Step 3: Add tasks to your organizational chart

Under each title, match a job description with the position. This exercise will help to streamline your organization by weeding out the inefficiencies, the duplicated tasks, and the forgotten tasks. Each task should also have a backup coordinator in case someone is out of the office for vacation, illness, or worse.

For a list of financial tasks to incorporate into the organizational chart and job descriptions, visit https://www.growthconsultingfirm.com/resources. You'll make this work for your business, although there are standards of practice.

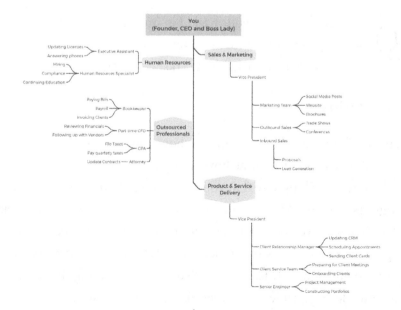

Step 4: Determine the amount of labor you can afford

Now that you've built your ideal organization let's take a look to see if you can afford your ideal organization. Consider the following factors when determining how much labor you can afford.

To follow along, check out the labor affordability worksheet on https://www.growthconsultingfirm.com/resources.

What is your hourly rate as the owner? If you bill your clients $400 an hour to do "big thinking" work, why do you do work that costs someone else much less? For example, can you hire someone to do your social media posts and content creation for $35 an hour? If you are doing your social media, and it takes an average of three hours a week, you are spending $1,200 of your precious billable time to do social media. If instead, you hire someone at $35 an hour, it will cost you $105 on average per week. That's a big savings; you can now fill those three hours with significant client work!

 Remember, I have your back! Go online to www.growthconsultingfirm.com/resources and download your Labor Worksheet today!

Labor Ratios

There are many ways to slice and dice how you look at anything in your company. Let's take a look at how well you are using your labor using actual metrics. Making sure that you have the right number of people (and the right people) working in your company is crucial to your success as an owner. If you have too many people, or the wrong people, then your company is at risk of wasting unnecessary dollars. Wasting money is sure fire way to go bankrupt. Remember that you are building the machine to be as valuable as possible for an eventual exit on your terms.

You can look at labor through a revenue lens, an overhead lens, an efficiency lens, and more. I will give you two ratios to use when dissecting your labor affordability.

Revenue per Employee = Total revenue ÷ by # Employees

Your answer to the above formula tells you how much revenue you can attribute to each employee. That includes you and anyone else on the payroll. You want this number to be as high as possible. Some of the most valuable Fortune 500 companies have upwards of $500,000 of revenue per employee. Realistically for small businesses less than ten million in annual revenue, this number will be much smaller. Aim for a revenue goal of $300,000 or more per employee. If you are not where you want it to be now, make a goal for the next quarter or year. If you want to hire someone, plug in the numbers as if you have already hired them.

Note: In our example, we are assuming that our next 12 months of revenue is staying the same.

For our organizational chart example above, let's assume we have nine admin employees.

CEO	Client Relationship Manager
HR Specialist	Client Service Team (2)
Executive Assistant	Senior Engineer
Sales & Marketing VP	Finance Team (2)
Marketing Team (2)	Junior Engineers (2)
Product & Service Delivery (2)	Operations (2)

Total Revenue last 12 months = $6,500,000 ÷ 18 = $361,111

$361,111 is a good amount of revenue generated per employee. Let's assume I would like to add two more employees. What would then happen to my revenue per employee ratio?

Total Revenue last 12 months = $6,500,000 ÷ 20 = $325,000

I encourage you to hire wisely. Make sure that when you hire, you are not hiring too quickly and seeing your revenue per admin employee significantly decrease. The lower amount, $325,000, is still a nice amount of revenue per employee, but I'm trending downward. Remember that every dollar you spend should have a return on investment. In this case, every employee you hire should improve your labor ratio. Maybe not right away, but definitely within 90 to 120 days. After hiring my two new employees, I want to look at this number every quarter to see if I'm improving my revenue per employee ratio. Even if I'm hiring a non-sales employee, such as an executive assistant or engineer, the hope is that I'm freeing up time for the CEO to generate more sales.

The second and one of the most common ways to analyze your labor is using the labor efficiency ratio.

Labor Efficiency Ratio =
Total Labor Costs ÷ Gross Revenue x100

In our previous example, let's assume that we have the following overhead costs for the past 12 months:

Payroll taxes	$272,000
Insurance	$187,000
Office Rent	$180,000
Employee Benefits	$199,000
Salaries	$820,000
Total	**$1,658,000**

Current Labor Efficiency Ratio = $1,658,000 ÷ $6,500,000 =
0.2632 x 100 = 25.5%

Ideally you want to bring in more sales with less labor. The rule of thumb is that, at most, 30 percent of your sales should go toward labor. In deciding whether or not you can afford to hire someone else, add the potential new hire's labor costs into this ratio. If your result is still less than 30 percent, that could be one more argument favoring hiring.

Our current labor efficiency ratio is less than 30 percent, which is on target. Let's say I want to add in those other two new hires, adding another $300,000 of overhead. My new ratio would then look like the following:

($1,658,000 + $300,000) ÷ $6,500,000 = 0.3232 x 100 = 30.1%

I've now gone above my 30 percent Labor Efficiency Ratio target. If you are not comfortable with this number, it's time to peel back the onion layers. I have a decision to make. Either I lower the cost of my labor all around, or I can be comfortable having a higher-than-expected labor ratio. A five percent difference might seem negligible, but I warn you that small changes anywhere in your finances can ripple throughout your business. If you are even slightly overspending, this affects all the company stakeholders. How can you reduce the cost of your total labor without compromising the integrity of your business?

Right now, go ahead and pause reading. I want you to go calculate your Labor Efficiency Ratio and Revenue per Employee number.

 Head over to www.growthconsultingfirm.com/resources to grab the Labor worksheet.

Contractor Costs

Depending on whom you talk to, some people think contractors can be cheaper in the long run, while others say contractors are more expensive. You have to make a cost comparison for the exact work that you want done.

As a rule of thumb, contractors should be about 25 percent higher than an employee's hourly wage because they own their overhead. You don't have to pay for insurance, rent, wages, taxes, etc. Your company's employee overhead could be much higher than 25 percent.

The total cost of labor depends on many factors. The operational difference between contractors and employees is in the control of the work. Ask yourself,

How much control do I want over the work itself?

As an owner, do I want to control the time, methods, and work structure? Or do I only care about the outcome of the work?

A contractor has full autonomy regarding how she works, where she works, and when. An employee does not have this same type of autonomy. An employee clocks in, clocks out, and has benefits and insurance that the company pays for. An employee can be subject to performance reviews.

By contrast, a contractor doesn't have to tell you how many hours she spent working on a project or when she worked. She's also not subject to performance reviews. You don't have control over her work methods.

Employee Costs

The total cost of an employee is not just the hourly wage. You must add to the cost:

- Payroll taxes
- Payroll processing fees
- Cost to find, interview, and onboard a new employee
- Insurance
- Overhead (office space, equipment, utilities)
- Employee benefits:
  - 401(k) or company-sponsored retirement plan
  - Vacation or family days, sick days
  - Additional insurance
  - Holiday parties
  - Other benefits such as childcare, student loan repayment
- Employee turnover: Loss of intellectual capital, client relationships, continuity
- Costs of hiring someone new: Added stress and workload to redistribute to other employees while you find a replacement, Learning curve

Monitoring the ROI on Your Team

Each department should track its contribution margin to the company. It's not enough that employees work day in and day out on projects when they don't know the bottom line. Communicate with your department heads so that they know

1. The cost of their overhead, labor, supplies, benefits, etc.
2. Their direct revenue
3. Their department profitability
4. Their proportion of contribution to the company's bottom line

Ensure you educate your employees on how and why this is important to the business. They should measure and track their information, reporting monthly to the CEO. As the CEO and Boss Lady, ensure you track your ROI and labor ratios over time. Be passionate about this number and obsess about the trends. Even if the ROI is not quite where you want it to be right now, that's OK. What matters is that you are making daily decisions that affect the bottom line and will help grow your team and your numbers.

Beyond your work team

Growing can be challenging, requiring business owners to step out of their comfort zones daily. Let's do an exercise together. Think back to the person you were when you started your business. Try to remember your personality, strengths, and weaknesses. Now think about where you are in your business right now. Picture yourself doing the work every day.

- How are you different now from when you started?
- Close your eyes and contemplate how you've changed.
- Where did you experience growth as a person?
- Was it painful? Was it fun?
- Did you discover something about yourself that surprised you?
- Where do you need to grow even more?

The business you are building is bigger than yourself. The skills needed to start your business will be different than the skills you need to survive growth in your business. And those skills will be different from the skills that you will need to find a successor. You know it's time to hire the right people to do the right work, whether they are employees or contractors. You also know it's time to get the right support structure around you, your A-team. Professionals who can help you, the owner, make the right moves and give you the right information to make the business even better and eventually sell it.

Your Informal Personal Advisory Board

Who do you go to when you have a problem running your business? You probably don't ask your employee for advice. You need to seek the counsel of wise people who have your best interest as a business owner. Who do you take out to coffee to pick their brain? Who do you call when you run into an issue? These are your informal advisory board members. You want to nourish them and keep them on speed dial. You could hold formal biannual meetings, but you don't have to make it formal. Approach your trusted friend and adviser to ask them to be your sounding board. You need at least two people, a maximum of five. Don't let too many cooks into the kitchen.

Another Business Owner

Learn from my mistakes! You need someone who has been a business owner in the past or is currently a business owner, someone with employees preferably. This person doesn't have to be in the same industry because the type of machine doesn't matter to your conversations. You are interested in learning from this person's business experience. They have great insight into the workings of a business and can see things from perspectives you may not have thought about. You should ask all sorts of operational or business questions of this person. You trust them to be discreet and not blab your business all about town.

A Friend

Sometimes you need someone to listen to you. Someone who will tell you that you have boogers coming out of your nose and not care about sparing your feelings. Someone who will tell you the truth to make you a better person. Likewise, you should be helping this friend become a better person. "Iron sharpens iron." This person is honest and kind. They could be a shoulder to cry on and don't necessarily have to help you solve your problems.

A Therapist

Friends are great, but they might not have the capacity to hear your sob stories repeatedly. Find a good mental health professional. Your sanity as the Boss Lady is paramount to the end. Some people will have to work through past traumas impacting their mental states. Other people will have anxieties and worries thrust upon them and won't know how to deal with them. You and I both will always have life's challenges to deal with. A therapist is a paid partner who will help you get the right tools for your tool belt so that you can be the best Boss Lady! Therapists are also bound by confidentiality and privacy laws.

A Technical Person

Find a person who is in the same industry as you. They don't have to be a business owner, but they should know your terminology, acronyms, and industry trends. You should feel comfortable talking about work with this technical person. The two of you can "geek out" on all the technical parts of the business in a judgment-free environment. A technical adviser can also help you bounce ideas around and find collaborative opportunities for the future.

A Connector

Everyone knows that person who knows everyone in town. She is the community connector. Do you have a leaky pipe? This person knows the perfect plumber. Do you need a good attorney? This person can give you five names. A connector is a valuable resource for you. "It's not what you know; it's who you know." A connector can help you get what you need at a moment's notice. Remember to nurture your connector, however. They thrive on new connections, so help them help you. Introduce your connector to new and exciting people you know. They'll end up talking about how great it was that you were the one that connected them. Who knows where those connections will lead? The world can be a small place.

Whoever is on your advisory board, ensure you take care of them. Their time is also precious, so don't make your meetings a gripe session. Don't use up their time. Give them a quick update on your business, then present the issue and ask for their advice. Send them thank you notes, small gifts, or help them in their business.

Case Study: The Passionate Boss Lady

Meet Corinna: She began her tech consulting business as a labor of love to help SMBs (small to medium businesses) implement technological strategies to give them a competitive advantage over larger corporations. She has a passion for helping these companies gain access to better ideas and better outcomes. Corinna has worked tirelessly over the past few years to build the company but has burned out. She works night and day and barely pays herself a living salary, even though she brings in about $3million of revenue each year. Fortunately, Corinna surrounds herself with a network of advisers and consultants she has personally curated over the past decade.

Corinna's Goals: She has many contractors working with her but only two employees. She's also unsure whether she spends money on the right projects or people. Corinna wants clarity on her financial life and a way to evaluate her current projects. She wishes to expand the company wisely and regain more time in her day. If she cannot rework her business, she fears that she will burn out entirely and quit the business she began.

Corinna's Obstacles: She does everything, from cleaning the toilets to delivering on her client work. She had a previous partner who took advantage of Corinna and the business, thus forcing Corinna to start over a few years ago. She trusts few people and prefers to do everything alone instead of building an internal team. Corinna's business would completely shut down if she left, even for a doctor's appointment.

Corinna's Outcome: Unfortunately, Corinna is like many other Boss Ladies I have met. She has worked for so many different people and placed herself last. We started first with trust-building. We needed to uncover why she was reluctant to hire employees. The story I shared above she revealed to me after many months of working together. Once we identified the reasons behind her current operating MO, we planned to repair the damage before moving on to the future.

We figured out what Corinna enjoyed doing with the business: building relationships, being a tech ambassador, and spreading her message. We uncovered what she hated about the business: bookkeeping, sales, marketing, and administrative work. Most importantly, we found trusted individuals who could work in the business while she worked on the business. She increased her revenue by over 250 percent, grew her profit margins, and went on a safari in Africa with her family, a bucket list item she never thought possible.

Finding the right team is challenging for an owner, but it is crucial for anyone wanting to grow. There will always be setbacks and disappointments, but that's part of the business.

Recently, I went to play poker with friends. I hadn't played poker in a long time, but I swept the house. My husband asked how I could win so many hands. It helped that many of these friends were new friends that didn't know my "tell." But I also believe that you win little if you risk little. If you risk much, even though there is potential to lose the house, there's also potential to win much. Business owners calculate risk. They know what they are working toward and are willing to take risks in hopes of a great reward. For Corinna, taking the risk of hiring someone was a big step, but the reward of more flexibility and time with her family was the huge win she was working for.

Section III:
Selling Your Business

Chapter 10

The Value of Your Business

I have two questions for you:

1. How much can you sell your business for — today?

2. How much do you need in order to move on to the next phase of life?

My hope for you is that you are not a statistic. As a woman business owner in the United States, the stats say you will fail to reach a million dollars in revenue. According to the Exit Planning Institute, eight out of 10 American business owners will not sell their business when it is time to leave the company.[10] The stats are wrong because you are reading this book, which means that you will be the one that does both – reach a million in revenue and sell the business (and look good while doing it).

You are the Boss Lady who drives the kids to volleyball practice, helps your aging parents, takes conference calls while walking the dog, hires employees, and attracts clients. You are the unicorn because you'll sell the business to the highest bidder at the end of your time in the company, then move on to the next chapter. So, how are you going to do that?

Selling a small or closely held business is an emotional event. I want you to take the emotion out of your business for this exercise altogether. I know that you were so passionate when you launched your business. I

---

[10] https://exit-planning-institute.org/state-of-owner-readiness

know you poured more blood, sweat, and tears into your business than at any other time in your career. Your company brand and goodwill in the community reflect your hard work and efforts. Your name or face might even be part of the brand identity.

However, taking the emotion out of the sale of your business can yield higher results for you and the new owners. I know that's easier said than done, so we will discuss the transactional value as well as the emotional journey of selling your small business.

The first thing we need to do is value your company. But let me tell you a secret: There is no right or wrong way to calculate your company's valuation. Every professional has a different spin on your valuation. Valuation is more like an art than an actual science because of the many moving parts and biases. You, the Boss Lady, get to decide what that calculation looks like. Different valuations of your company will become a basis for negotiation. You get an expert's opinion on what they think your business is worth. It is an opinion based on facts and observations but still just an opinion.

Having an accurate valuation that can hold up in court is a worthwhile exercise, although it costs you a pretty penny. You can then take that opinion to the bank, an investor, a partner, or a buyer. It's then up to the other party to prove that opinion wrong.

Each expert will have their reasoning and basis for determining their opinion. For example, a CPA might value your firm based on one method and come up with an opinion of $7.5 million. A valuation expert might come up with a value of $9.2 million. A business broker might only give you a calculation of $5.9 million.

As the Boss Lady, you get to decide which opinion is closest to your perceived value, then use that as the beginning of your negotiations.

I'll illustrate the main types of calculations used when valuing a business. Remember these are generic themes meant to illustrate an idea for you. Within a formal valuation, there can be thousands of calculations. Do not take this as legal advice; get a professional's opinion.

Types of Valuation Calculations

How much can you sell your business for today?

DCF: Discounted Cash Flow

Take a trip down memory lane with me back to high school math class. Today's dollar is not worth the same as it will be in 10 years. Likewise, a dollar is worth more today than five years ago. The "time value of money" is one of the most used methods of valuing a company. DCF takes the cash your business generates into the future, then brings that value back to today's numbers. This method takes the total of projected future cash flows and "discounts" it back to the present value.

Below, I will give you the concepts and the basic formula. It's not my intention to walk you through the calculations because if so, I'm sure your head might start spinning backward unless you are an engineer or math wizard. Pay attention to the concepts rather than the formulas. By design, I did not make a corresponding worksheet for this chapter, so just read on through and take notes for now.

The Process:

Step 1 – "Recast" (aka "normalize") your profit & loss statement

- Find your Net Income (the Cash Flow, *C*)
- Remove any expenses that won't transfer to a new owner.
  - (Expenses like payroll for your cousin who doesn't do much, a private jet to transport the owner, company parties, and more of these discretionary type of expenses.)
- Remove non-recurring expenses
  - Non-recurring expenses like a one time trip to a conference or flowers delivered to an employee in the hospital.
- Remove income that is not a part of your core operations
- Add realistic taxes and realistic owner compensation

Step 2 – Determine the number of years of future viability

- Period of time, *N*
  - How many more years can your company be in business, realistically?

Step 3 – Research a viable Discount Rate, *r*

- What's the weighted average cost of capital (WACC) for your business? WACC is the return that an outside investor should expect to receive from lending your company money.

Assumptions used in the discounted cash flow model:

- The Rate of growth in future years is constant, each year you will presumedly have linear growth instead of the usual ups and downs.

- The discount for riskier companies should be higher than conservative companies.
- The business's value is the present value of future cash flows.
- Base calculations are through annual time periods.
- The business does not go on forever, so we use an ending date range.
- The value r is the required rate of return.

Formula for calculating DCF:

$$V = \sum_{i=1}^{N} \frac{C_i}{(1+r)^i}$$

Can also be written as...

Your Business Value =
(Cash Flow Year)¹ + (Cash Flow Year)² + (Cash Flow Year)³ + ...

$$(1+r) \qquad (1+r)^2 \qquad (1+r)^3$$

The Emotions: Start-up business owners often have crazy, wild forecasts for their business. They don't have any history to justify their calculations, but they are confident that they can break even Year 1. Year 2 will be the year that they have a 10 percent rate of return. Year 3 is when they get to an ROE of 35 percent, and so on. I love that they are so passionate about their business. Established business owners often don't have the same unfounded expectations. However, they can still run into problems when they assume wild rates of return for future forecasting. Some owners have over-inflated expectations of their company's potential. It's always best to be more conservative with your numbers. Hope for the best, but plan for the worst.

Any type of projection like this is an opportunity to play around with the numbers on paper, without any real-life consequences. Be conservative with your assumptions and then back fill the activities and plans that go into this projection. For example, assume that you calculate a lower Discounted Cash Flow value. Dissect the net income each year and see what you can change to increase your valuation. Are your expenses too high? Can you bring in more or different streams of revenue? Strategy is the real beauty of the DCF number, or any other forward-looking projection. Use the DCF projections to play around with possibilities.

Comparisons

How do you compare to other businesses in your industry? Buyers will want to know why they should buy your company over all other similar types of businesses that do what you do. They will compare your business in a fair and objective manner. It's a very "sterile" process that once again takes the emotion out of the calculation. Analysts will use a concept called a "multiple" that shows the buyer how your business does relative to similar companies. While this is a seemingly simple method of valuing your company, it requires some complex concepts. Again, don't try and value your company this way alone. You'll need to get professional help to determine the appropriate analysis. The process outlined below is a simplistic overview of a complicated calculation in order to provide you the education you need to have enlightened conversations.

Process for Comparisons:

Step 1 - Find your EBITDA.

Step 2 - Find several comparable companies.

Step 3 - Average the comparable companies' multiples.

Step 4 - Multiply your EBITDA by this average.

Step 5 - Adjust your result from Step 4 by any discounts.

Step 6 - Adjust your result from Step 5 by adding any premiums.

Assumptions:

- We are comparing privately owned companies to privately owned companies, not publicly traded companies.
- Comparable companies may not be the same in revenue, number of employees, risk, and other business characteristics.
- The multiple we use in our calculation should be an average of several similar businesses.
- Your company's multiple might be very different from the industry standard.

Formula:

Your Business Value \$ = EBITDA x Multiple

Step 1 – Find your EBITDA

EBITDA: Earnings Before Interest Taxes Deductions and Amortization

Say it with me, "Eee-bit-daaaaaah." What are your company's earnings before you take out the interest, taxes, and depreciation? This number isn't readily available on your P&L but start with the line on your P&L that says, "Net Operating Income." Depreciation and amortization are on your Statement of Cash Flows, which you'll need to add back in to your Net Operating Income.

EBITDA = Net Operating Income + Interest + Taxes + Depreciation + Amortization

Step 2 – Find several comparable companies

Look at other companies that do what you do, the same way you do it, and look and smell the same as you. Look for companies with similar products, services, customer base, revenue, location, and employee size. Check out your NAICS code and look at valuation reference books or online resources to see similar companies. You can go to your library or get with a valuation expert to find what similar NAICS businesses have sold for over the past few years.

Step 3 – Average the comparable companies' multiples

Likely, you'll find a range of multiples, from 1 to 10. You are a small, private business, so looking at a publicly traded company to find this information will take a lot of work. It's like comparing apples to onions. You can compare your privately held business to a publicly traded company, but it requires peeling back the onion layers and looking at other ratios to find the exact number. Once you find a handful of similar companies, calculate the average of these their multiples.

Step 4 – Multiply your EBITDA by the answer from Step 3

Your EBITDA x Average Comparable Multiple

Step 5 – Adjust your result from Step 4 by any discounts

Discount your result from the previous step back to reality. The reality is that only a few businesses are ready to transfer that value to a new owner. The value to the new owner is less than your value today. How can you ensure a seamless transfer of ownership with the least number of bumps and setbacks possible?

Analysts call this the lack of marketability. In a perfect world all companies would have all the information and processes together to protect and continue the business. This includes proper insurance, buy/sell agreements, employee manuals, documented workflows, updated contracts with vendors, clients, and employees, and many other tasks that must be a part of your daily operating life. The transfer of ownership to a new buyer would be smooth if you had all of these in place and up to date. The reality is that many small businesses don't actually have everything in place and up to date. Hence, we must "discount" your valuation because your business is not perfectly marketable.

Think of your business like a home that is up for sale. You might have had the walls painted inside to look good, but the water heater is 15 years old and the roof is going to need to be replaced. These are tasks that the new owner will most likely have to do if they buy the home. A buyer might argue that your asking price is too high based on the amount of work that needs to be done on the home.

For example:

Step 4: EBITDA $4,000,000 x Multiple of 3.5 = Value of $14,000,000

Step 5: Value of $14,000,000 minus a 55% discount = Value of $6,300,000

A buyer that goes through the due diligence process of purchasing your company will likely only pay about $6.3 million, not the $14 million that you were hoping for.

Imagine a horse-pulled wagon filled with piles and piles of gold coins. There are so many gold coins in this wagon that it's overflowing. What would happen to all those gold coins if that horse (or probably more like a group of horses) were to pull the wagon right now? More than likely, the coins will fall right out of the wagon.

What if you put a net or burlap sheets over the top of the wagon? Would you lose the same number of coins? How many coins would you lose if you securely put them in wooden or metal boxes before loading them onto the wagon?

Think of your business as gold coins. You are putting your business value into the wagon to send to the new owner. If you want to transfer the same value to a new owner, you must ensure it doesn't fall out of the wagon during the transfer. The risk in the transfer process is that the new business will not do well in the new owner's hands. Customers might lose service, or employees may not get paid. Think of the processes, insurance, manuals, and up-to-date policies as the burlap net. If I were a new owner, I would ensure you had these processes (or metal vaults) in place before I purchased your company.

But don't stop there!

Step 6 – Adjust your result from Step 5 by adding any premiums

Premium add-ins: Some aspects of your business are hard, if not impossible, to value. No mathematical formula exists to determine the value of intangible assets such as brand awareness, goodwill, and reputation. Some consulting agencies try to place a number on these intangibles, but it's difficult at best. Sometimes you can quantify it by looking at the number of email subscribers, survey results, or other methods. However, those methods will never truly quantify how well-loved your brand is in your community or what your reputation says to customers.

Fortunately, you do have a say when it comes to this. **If** you can back up your logic, you can add a premium to your business value.

How much are the following items worth?

- Customer lists
- Employee loyalty
- Brand recognition
- Your company's goodwill
- Contracts
- And more!

Example:

Step 4: EBITDA $4,000,000 x Multiple of 3.5 = Value of $14,000,000

Step 5: Value of $14,000,000 minus a 55% discount = Value of $6,300,000

Step 6: Value of $6,300,000 + Premium Add-ins of $1,200,000 = Final Transferrable Value of $7,500,000

While this final value is still far from your $14 million EBITDA, it's good to know how much transferrable value you've built into the company. Going through this exercise is also a great way to find out what you need to work on in the company in order to increase the transferrable value. Pay attention to the things that discounted your company from its original comparable value. If you have time before selling to a buyer (ideally before a buyer ever approaches you) try to work on addressing those discounts. Having all of your ducks in a row is not only great to increase the value of your business, it's also great to increase operating efficiency and decrease risk within your organization!

*Note: Remember that much of your final transferable value you will lose to taxes, depending on which transfer method you finally settle on.

The Emotions

I've heard so many owners over the years tell me that their multiple is much higher than it truly is. They base this assumption on their neighbor's friend's business, which is kind of like theirs (but not really). That neighbor's friend sold their company for a seven multiple, so that's what they will expect because they're obviously better than their neighbor's friend. I'm exaggerating, but that's a typical story that I hear. Don't let pride get in the way of seeing your business for what it is. I know that your business is like your baby, but sometimes your business needs to be objectively looked at for what it is, not what you want it to be.

Liquidation Value aka Book Value aka Balance Sheet Method

Many CPAs will begin a valuation analysis by looking at the balance sheet to determine the worst-case scenario. If you cannot find a buyer for your business for the amount you would like, or if you don't have time to find a buyer, how much could you recoup? Unfortunately, many liquidation sales happened during the pandemic. Some small business owners needed more time or resources to sell their business for the value it was worth. They had to sell because of their health or financial situation during the lockdown. These owners sold their business assets one by one, paid any remaining debts, then kept the left-over cash, if there was any cash left.

In other cases, a liquidation sale is an absolutely viable possibility that could be higher than the other types of valuation. For instance, a construction firm that has a specialized niche in what they provide. The specialty has never been documented and the original founder has long since passed away. Other competitors have copied their work and entered the marketplace. For this type of company, a liquidation sale might yield a much higher valuation than a DCF or comparison value.

Liquidation Process:

Step 1	Pull up your balance sheet from last month.
Step 2	Identify each asset for sale, everything from printers and trucks to real estate.
Step 3	Identify the current market value for each asset.
Step 4	Sell the individual assets.
Step 5	Pay off all liabilities.
Step 6	Distribute any remaining amounts to the shareholders / owners.

Assumptions:

- You sell assets to the highest bidder.
- Assets are no longer used to generate cash flow.
- Use an appraiser, if necessary
- Balance sheet asset values may not be indicative of current market values.
- Business operations will cease immediately.

Formula: Your Business Value = Assets - Liabilities

The Emotions

The liquidation valuation can be a disappointing event because it assumes your business will close forever. However, it doesn't have to be the worst-case scenario. The book value valuation is often a viable solution for many owners. One Boss Lady of a construction firm told me there was "no way in hell" that she would ever sell her company to a buyer when she retired. She did not want another owner to drag her excellent name through the mud by changing everything she worked so hard for. She prided herself on the company's operations and brand recognition in the community. She wanted to avoid tarnishing her goodwill if a bad manager purchased her business.

Still, COVID-19 forced other owners into this position. They didn't have an exit strategy and had to close the business in a hurry. These owners unintentionally left millions of dollars on the table by having a liquidation sale, but they had no other choice. If this is the method you decide to use, that's OK. But you need to plan for it. Whatever method you decide, remember that the goal is to get the *most* value from your business, to reap the highest amount you can.

Why You Need to Know Your Business Valuation

How much do you need to move on to the next chapter?

Let's look at this whole valuation concept from a different angle.

One day, you might not be able to walk to the toilet, remember to eat, or sadly even remember who the good-looking person is in front of you. In the insurance world, these are ADLs, or Activities of Daily Living. You will need someone to care for you because if you live to a ripe old age, you can't care for yourself, let alone anyone else.

Back up a few years before this, however. When you retire, you'll want to sit on a beach somewhere, travel the world, start a nonprofit, care for the grandkids, or do any other number of unique goals. You won't bring in the dough anymore, though. You'll be spending all that hard-earned, well-deserved cash. In the financial world we call this the "decumulation" stage: You are spending down your assets.

Your challenge today is to figure out where this hard-earned cash will come from. As a business owner, you may not have the luxury to draw from the traditional pension, and Social Security sure won't be enough to let you sail into the sunset. In fact Social Security was never meant to be a retirement plan for everyone, but that's a soap box for another book.

Traditional financial planning looks at your current assets today, your goals for tomorrow, and tries to determine some routes that bridge the gap between the two. Work with a financial planner to track down your sources of income during retirement, what you need in retirement, and any "gaps" in your plan.

For example, a marketing guru calculated her Social Security, an old pension, and a rental property that will provide her with about $120k a year during retirement. She figured out that her living expenses will decrease from what they are now to about $180k a year in retirement. This total includes groceries, travel, real estate taxes for three properties, gifts for the grandchildren, hobbies, and more. However, she still needs to account for long-term care because she doesn't want to burden her children. She would also like to leave a small inheritance behind to her grandkids. This Boss Lady must factor in the value of her marketing company sale as well.

Through additional savings in her old retirement plans, she decided that she will need about a 4.5 percent withdrawal rate from her assets in the first 10 years of retirement, then about a 3.1 percent withdrawal rate every year after that to supplement her living expenses. A good financial planner can tell you what you need to do to maintain your lifestyle and plan for all the "what-ifs" in life to self-insure through your savings and the building up of your assets.

While accumulating assets, it is a good idea to plan how your business will fit into your financial plan. Calculate the amount you need from the sale of your business (after taxes).

Using our previous example: You have a final value of $7,500,000 minus taxes. You determined that you must sell the company for at least $9,000,000. That's a shortfall of $1,500,000.

Your business is $1.5 million shorter than you need it to be. How do you grow this business of yours by $1.5 million in the next few years before you retire or move on to the next chapter? How can you squeeze any more juice out of your lemon? Can you get any extra value out of your business, given that you are still tirelessly sweating away day after day?

How to Increase the Value of Your Business – Putting in the work, again

The good news is that it is possible to increase the value of your business by addressing key areas if you have time and plan in advance. You probably have some of these started or at least know about them intellectually. This next section will walk you through items that will help. Remember to put on your "buyer's" hat and think about the transferable value of your business from the other side of the table.

Owner Independent

If you can't take a vacation for two weeks without checking your phone every five seconds for a business issue, then your company is 100 percent dependent on you as the owner to be there.

The company should run without you because if it can't, the business will never grow beyond you.

Getting the business to run without your presence will add tremendous value to your company. Remember that you are making your business a machine.

- Hire the right people, fire the wrong people.

- Let go of your baggage, whether it's distrusting people, control issues, or anything else that could get in the way of scaling your business.

- Write down all the processes and procedures in an operating manual. The goal is to transfer all the knowledge from your brain into a stranger's brain off the street, with minimal impact during the transition.

Diversify, Diversify, Diversify

Diversify your customer base and never let one or two customers make up most of your revenue. What happens if that one customer goes away? Will your business still survive? Will you have enough revenue to pay the bills? How long will you stay afloat if your largest client leaves you?

Diversify your supply vendors. Never allow another company to dictate how and when you fulfill customer obligations. Have backup suppliers and negotiate contracts annually, at the least. As I type this paragraph, people worldwide are still recovering from the supply chain issues of the pandemic.

Diversify your talent pool. Don't be afraid to diversify the people that you surround yourself with. If everyone in your company looks and smells the same, the chances are they think the same as well. I never shy away from what some people call confrontation. Disagreements can be a beautiful space to innovate and create something new that is lasting and solid. The more different the ideas you hear, the more you can build up your empathy muscles and see situations from unique perspectives. Life would be so boring if we were all built the same.

Make it "Sticky"

Once your vendors, customers, and employees are in place, get a good attorney to draft some "sticky" long-term contracts that protect both yourself and the customer. Buyers will pay a premium if they know they can't lose a client after taking over your company. Also, make sure the contracts are transferable to a new buyer. Sometimes this is an overlooked item.

Ensure that everyone wants to keep coming back to your business. Customers should love your brand and your services. Think of Apple; it sells iPhones, iPads, watches, and more. Many Apple customers are big fans of the culture and the products. Suppliers want to work with Apple. Employees want to work at Apple. Make your company sticky, and it will increase your business's value.

Through your hard work, you can close that $1.5 million gap by increasing your company's value. You will have an up-to-date operating manual, diverse staff, and recurring customers. You've locked in clients with ironclad contracts, and your customer service keeps them returning for more. Your company is now worth the $9 million you dreamed of! Retirement is just around the corner, and you can already taste the pina coladas waiting for you on the beach.

Case Study: The Exiting Owner

Meet Esther: Esther is a doctor by day and a business owner by night. She is a partner in a successful medical practice and does a procedure that few doctors perform. She is in high demand, especially in the past few years because she has perfected her craft. By night, Esther is 51 percent owner of a very successful business with her brother. This business has been rapidly growing during the past decade, and she feels reluctantly compelled to work on the business more. Esther is married in her late 50s, and her kids are out of the house.

Esther's Goals: Esther wants to spend more time with her husband and travel the world. She is considering transitioning into medical teaching to raise the next generation of experts. She also wants to exit her business with her brother but doesn't want to disappoint him. She is expecting her first grandchild in a few months and wants to be available to help. Esther worries that her income will drop too much if she semi-retires, and she wants to know how to see her projected cash flow.

Esther's Obstacles: Time is scarce, especially for Esther and everything she wants to accomplish. She doesn't know how to prioritize, nor does she have any clue about where she stands financially. Her business with her brother is scaling too quickly, and they have cash flow problems. Other states are calling her to perform her medical procedures on high-risk patients. She feels stressed, and her health is starting to show it.

Esther's Outcome: Esther came to me by referral and was in a panic. She needed someone to help her quickly. However, her schedule and fast-paced lifestyle made it challenging to communicate with her and get the information I needed to help her accomplish her goals. Once we had a heart-to-heart conversation, Esther turned over a brand-new leaf. She knew that she had to prioritize her financial affairs if she was ever going to get off the hamster wheel.

We spent the next few months organizing her financial life, analyzing her position in the business, and cleaning up what we could. Initially, she thought she had to sell the business to her brother, but their buy/sell agreement was in dire need of an update, and he lacked the cash to buy her out anyway. Fortunately, the business was very profitable, and Esther could sign for a loan for her brother to buy out her share of the company. Esther now sits on the board of advisers for her brother and even advises him on his own eventual exit from the company. She retired from the medical practice and now teaches at a medical school in California. Esther is semi-retired now and plans to travel abroad at least once a year with her husband and spend time with her grandchildren.

Chapter 11

Investing: Scale Beyond the Business

Business owners are different types of investors. They take calculated risks to begin a business. It takes guts to forego a steady paycheck in exchange for a world of uncertainty. Instead, a funny thing happens after they start their first business. Some business owners become serial investors, putting their resources into various ventures, real estate, and other investments to grow over time. Yet many times the investments continue beyond just one company. Whatever you decide to invest in, developing a personalized investment policy statement is critical to keep you focused and prioritized.

Corporations and nonprofit entities often have an IPS that board members and executives refer to. Imagine a conference room with various board members seated around the table. They have come together for a meeting to decide what to do with the entity's extra cash. The board decided that the extra cash is unnecessary for the foreseeable future, and they don't have expansion plans. They agree to put the money to work and earn a higher return. The board members come from various backgrounds, education, and jobs. Their opinions on what the investments should be are quite different from each other. Diversity is a great feature within a company, but without guidelines for the board members to follow, chaos can ensue at the organization's expense.

The same goes for your company. Without a guide for your investments, you may get sidetracked, unable to decide, make the wrong decision, miss critical pieces to your investment portfolio, or overlap pieces without even realizing it.

An Investment Policy Statement helps you to avoid emotional investing.

Writing out your policy says a lot about your discipline and procedures when investing. Without an IPS (Investment Policy Statement), you can perhaps overlook priorities or put them to the bottom of the list. An IPS also takes much of the emotion out of investing. Inexperienced investors can feel tempted to buy high and sell low at the whims of what the media says or what their neighbors pressure them to do.

This chapter will walk through the basic thought processes behind an IPS and show you how to write one for your accounts and your business accounts. We'll discuss what types of investments belong in your portfolio and which ones may not suit you. At the end of the exercise, you can articulate your investment philosophies and have a path forward.

 Visit https://www.growthconsultingfirm.com/resources to download a template.

Step 1: Know Yourself

1. Your Net Worth

The first thing you must do is take inventory of all your current assets and liabilities. We need a detailed list of your net worth. List the type of asset, the value, the rate of return, the title of the asset, beneficiaries, the location, and any other relevant information. Doing so will give you a deeper look into what you have.

You'll avoid:

- Unintentional duplicate investments
- Losing the asset or neglecting the asset
- Mental accounting that leads to incorrect math

You'll gain:

- Regular clarity on the asset's effectiveness and place in your portfolio

- Pride in seeing your asset list evolve over time

- Efficiencies that perhaps you couldn't see before

Next come the liabilities. On the same spreadsheet, list the liabilities for you or your business. List mortgages, credit cards, personal and business loans, and more. Track the account balance, interest rate, titling, due dates, and payments. Many people like to avoid their liabilities and not look at their statements or other reminders. I say to face them head-on! Track your liabilities and decide whether it's worth keeping the balance to leverage your company or if the debt is unsecured and has no place in your portfolio. Pay it off and be done with it. See Chapter 7, Debt & Capital Expenditures, to revisit how to pay off your unsecured debt.

Your **Net Worth** is the number that remains when you subtract the total liabilities from your total assets. Track your net worth at least once a year during tax season. Some clients have loved seeing their net worth go up and down and therefore track it more frequently. If you do that, don't be surprised if your net worth decreases because of market or economic fluctuations.

2. Your Risk Capacity

How much is at risk? What percentage of your total portfolio would that investment represent if you were to invest in something right now? For example,

Assets	
Your Company	$2,500,000 (58%)
Old 401(k)	$650,000 (15%)
Cash Account	$45,000 (1%)
Primary Residence	$1,000,000 (23%)
Savings Account	$120,000 (3%)
Total	**$4,315,000 (100%)**

A new investment opportunity has come up, and you've decided to use $100,000 from your savings account to invest in this opportunity. Your new asset list would look like this:

Assets	
Your Company	$2,500,000 (58%)
Old 401(k)	$650,000 (15%)
Cash Account	$45,000 (1%)
Primary Residence	$1,000,000 (23%)
Savings Account	$20,000 (.5%)
New Investment	$100,000 (2.5%)
Total	**$4,315,000 (100%)**

Could you take a different risk with something 0.5 percent of your overall net worth than 58 percent of your total net worth? If this new investment completely flops, will your portfolio withstand the loss? That's up to you to decide. Write the answer down as part of your IPS.

3. Your Appetite for Risk

Speaking of market fluctuations, how many ups and downs can you stomach? Are you the type of person who can look at a significant decrease in your portfolio, say about 20 percent down in a single day, and still be OK with where your money is invested? Or are you the type of person who prefers less volatility and wouldn't like to see your portfolio decline more than 5 percent?

Raise your hand right now if you want to see your investments increase 20 percent in a month. I'm hopeful that everyone raised their hands just now. Of course, we all want to see gains in our investments. But sometimes those gains come with more significant declines. Which mix are you?

- How would you describe your investment risk tolerance?

- What do the words conservative or aggressive mean to you?

- Do you identify more with moderate investments?

While these words can have very different meanings for everyone, it is a beginning step to truly understanding your underlying thought processes.

Each type of investment comes with its own general risk and reward profile. You must match your investment to your goal, and each goal should have a unique blend of investments. A typical investment vehicle you may hear about is called a Target Date Fund. These are usually investments for large employer-sponsored retirement plans, like your old 401(k). An employee can pick a target date fund that coincides with her planned retirement age. For example, I could pick a target date of 2040 when I hope to retire, or better yet a target date of 2065 when I hope to begin pulling money out of the account.

As I save money into my 401(k) account, I invest the money into this 2040 target date fund. In 2020, the fund may include investments like smaller companies, brand-new businesses, international stock, and other riskier but potentially profitable investments. But as time passes, the fund will become increasingly more conservative. In the year 2035, the 2040 target date fund might be more government bonds than growth stocks. The fund wants to preserve the money in the investments because I'll be pulling the money out of the fund soon.

Step 2: Know Your Goals

Revisit your goals in the first chapter of this book. When considering your investments, remember the various goals you wish to accomplish using these opportunities. For example, are you investing to send your child to college in a few years? Are you investing because you want to own the building that your company headquarters is in? What are your goals?

We'll use college as an example. I have two children who I want to send to a four-year college each. I'm unsure exactly where they will go, but we'll assume an in-state public university.

1. **Assign a value to the goals**: How much will your goal cost you in today's dollars? How much is college for your kids today? How much do you need to live on in the future when you are no longer earning an income?

   In our example, let's assume that each child needs about $50,000 a year to attend a state university.

2. **Look at the timeline**: How long before you need to reach that goal? Retirement might be another 16 years for you. But college for the kids might come sooner.

Child 1 will begin college in three years.

Child 2 will begin college in seven years.

3. **Add annual inflation**: Using today's dollars for each goal, forecast the expense out into the future.

   Child 1 will need about $56,000 for the first year of college, increasing annually at about 4 percent for inflation.

   Child 2 will need about $63,000 for the first year of college, increasing about 4 percent annually for inflation.

Your timeline is important because investments that coincide with a short-term goal will vastly differ from those you use for a long-term goal. As a rule of thumb, short-term goals should be less risky and less volatile. The reason is that you need more time to recoup any losses you may incur. Using our college example from the previous paragraph, if you must send your child to college for the next three years, you may want to avoid putting their college tuition fund into a brand-new start-up. Instead, you might want to invest in safer instruments like CDs or short-term bonds. Yes, the return will be very little, if anything, but you will not risk the principal balance. Your child will depend on that tuition check, and universities usually require cash up front.

On the other hand, if you are investing for your retirement vacation home in 20 years, you can invest in any other number of highly volatile investments. The potential for high returns is there, and if you have a few down years, you still have the potential to make it up because you have two decades to reach that goal.

Once you know where you stand with your current assets and liabilities as an investor and have clarity on your goals, you can begin to build your investment portfolio. Your IPS should clearly state what you can and cannot invest in as an individual. Write these all down to build your IPS.

Step 3: Restricted investments[11]

Cryptocurrency is a highly debated asset in the United States. Before the fall of FTX, I heard about many clients who wanted to dabble in crypto because they had a friend of a neighbor of a friend who "made lots of money" by investing in crypto. I know many spouses of these clients who firmly oppose any investments in crypto for the family's portfolio. We also often forget or never hear about those investors who did invest but lost their life savings.

A hundred years ago, people avoided "sin stocks" as investments. A sin stock is an investment in a company or industry that some consider immoral or unethical, such as tobacco, alcohol, weapons, etc. Although these investments tend to do better than others during a recession or down market, some investors try to avoid them.

Nowadays, the buzzword is "ESG" (Environmental, Social, and Governance) investing. Some investors want to invest in companies doing well in these categories. As I write this, the SEC (Securities and Exchange Commission) and others in our country are debating what ESG really means, what the standards should be, and if advisers are negligent by telling clients to invest in ESG. Many times ESG companies perform subpar to other companies, which might make them a less than desirable

---

[11] This is not to be constituted as investment advice. It's for illustration and educational purposes only. Consult your financial professional. All investments assume risk. Past performance is not indicative of future returns. Consider all fees and negative returns before investing in any asset.

investment. You should do your due diligence and research these investments if this is part of your IPS.

If you fall into either of these categories, make sure your IPS reflects clearly what you can and cannot invest in. When the next trend or "fad" comes on the market, you can refer to your policy to determine if it aligns with your values and goals.

The IPS is the first step to investing. Deciding what to invest in is the next step. I recommend that you hire someone who does this for a living. They can help you craft an IPS and customize an investment portfolio best suited to your needs and lifestyle; research a "fee-only" financial advisor for a fiduciary who has your best interest in mind.

You can't know *what* to invest in if you don't know *why* you are investing!

Case Study: The New CEO

Meet Joni: She is a *boss*! A former military turned hard charging and successful employee of a large Fortune 1000 firm. Her former boss recently retired, and she became CEO in a never-before-seen environment of unanimous support from the Board of Directors and her peers. Joni has two children in college; her husband is a retired executive. Her father recently passed away, and she is now taking care of her aging mother.

Joni's Goals: Joni has been taking care of the family's finances for decades, including her grandparents' estate and all the investment management for her family. She wants to get a professional set of eyes on her investments to see if she's missing anything. Joni also has other questions about insurance, taxes, and what she should do with her pay raise.

She hopes to retire in 10 years, but her personal Excel spreadsheets aren't telling her a great story.

Joni's Obstacles: She was taking over an organization amidst the global pandemic, and she doesn't have much time to dedicate to her finances as she did in the past. But she is also reluctant to give up the reins because she's done things her way for a long time.

Joni's Outcome: Joni is well organized, a careful leader, inspirational, and analytical. While she had done a great job organizing her financial life, we found some discrepancies. For example, Joni claimed to be an "aggressive" investor, but her investments were very conservative. We realigned her investments with her true risk tolerance by developing a customized investment policy statement.

We implemented a financial plan that immediately showed her how she could retire now instead of ten years from now if she chose to do so and still maintain the quality of life she wanted. Joni could sleep well at night because she knew her finances were in order. We built a strategy that included care for her mom, her children and her husband — and even some luxury vacations every couple years! Knowing her personal balance sheet and investment policy statement meant that she was in control of her decisions and had flexibility.

Joni has achieved her dream of being financially independent. If you ask her what that means, she will gladly tell you that it's the flexibility to continue working or stop working. She shows up to work daily because she wants to, not because she must. This newfound luxury changed her mentality and leadership and brought so much joy to her life!

Chapter 12

Your Legacy: More than a Boss Lady

The Merriam-Webster dictionary defines a legacy[12] as a gift, something transmitted or received from an ancestor.

When I was a kid, I loved getting gifts on Christmas. I loved opening the wrapping paper and seeing what beautiful new toy awaited me under the tree. As is the case with many people when they age, material objects don't bring me as much joy as they used to. I prefer to share experiences with people I love — going on adventures, making memories, and telling stories. I still love watching my daughters open their birthday or Christmas gifts, but I expect that one day they will love the gift of an experience more than they love a toy or material item.

What legacy do you wish to transmit to the people who you will leave behind? More likely than not, your current business has an element of legacy. You've poured your heart and soul into the business because you want the business to carry on without you one day. The fact that potentially selling the business to fund your lifestyle and goals for the next chapter is just icing on the cake. You've been the Boss Lady for a while now, but you know you are more than that. The title, "Boss Lady," isn't big enough to hold your entire heart. You have dreams beyond your current business.

---

[12] https://www.merriam-webster.com/dictionary/legacy

**What actually motivates you isn't just the money;
it's the legacy.**

If you don't know your legacy, let me suggest a few ways to find it.

Author Simon Sinek talks about finding your motivation in his book
called *Start with Why* (Portfolio, 2009). Sinek suggests that the why is the
powerful motivator to get you to see past the superficial success of
achievement. I beg to differ! We are on this Earth to nurture relationships.
I believe that our "why" is actually our "who." Look for your "who." In
your life, take stock of who is important to you. Your children, your
spouse, your friends, your employees, your customers — and even you,
yourself. Each "why" you could ever think of is actually backed by a
person. Your company is ultimately supporting the people that are most
important to you.

I wrote this book for my daughters, first and foremost. I believe in my
heart that they are meant to do great work for this world. I want them to
know how to navigate the business world better than I did when I started.
I'm passing on my GPS, so they don't have to drive a stick shift with a
giant folded paper map in LA traffic in the '90s. (Yes, mom was born
before the internet, kids!)

I also wrote this book for the other "mompreneurs" who are cleaning up
poopy diapers, taking conference calls in the laundry room, and don't
have time to wash their hair, let alone get a degree in economics. Their
families rely on them, and they are working their butts off. Studies have
shown that the mother in the family usually dictates the education level

and even the spiritual beliefs of the household.[13] These women deserve first-class support, not sloppy seconds.

I'm building my business to support the women who have made it past a million dollars in revenue, defied gravity, and crashed through the glass ceiling. They're tired but can see the light at the end of the tunnel. I'm here to help them achieve their dreams and cross the finish line with dignity.

I'm building my business to one day give back to my community in huge and impactful ways. I can't do what I want to do on the salary of an employee. My "who" needs more than that. I feel blessed to live in this modern age with running water in my home and meal delivery at my fingertips. I also believe we are all stewards of wealth and that our wealth is a privilege. With this privilege comes great responsibility (mo' money, mo' problems) to give back to our communities and leave the world in a better state than we entered.

I am creating waves in the financial industry because I am tired of sitting to the side, marginalized and ignored. I'm tired of someone telling me my resume must be fake because it's too good to be true, that women don't care about finances, and that I shouldn't speak my mind. In the worksheet below, list the "who's" in your life. Who did you start your business for? Why did you start your business? Who are you trying to support?

 Head over to https://www.growthconsultingfirm.com/resources to download the legacy worksheet.

---

[13] http://www.jstor.org/stable/2765006

Legacy Worksheet

WHO	Reason	My Legacy
My daughters	To make their journey easier	Business acumen that continues to grow, resilience in the face of adversity, dedication to giving back
My community	To make a large and lasting impact	
Other women business owners		

You've identified the "what" (your business) and the "who" (see above worksheet). Let's talk about the "how." How can you pass on your legacy? How do you leave your mark on this world? Below are a few ideas you can consider. Always seek legal and expert advice on applying these to your situation.

Trusts

My words here are in no way legal or tax advice. Please consult your attorney or tax professional for further details regarding your situation. This book is for illustration purposes only.

There are many kinds of trusts out there, such as CLAT, CRUT, GRIT, GRAT, RLT, ILT, and many more. The type of name tells the reader what the intention of the trust accomplishes. For example, a CLAT is a Charitable Lead Annuity Trust where a charity receives recuring payments while the grantor is alive. Once the grantor of the trust passes, the remaining balance goes to the named beneficiary. Many times, these are wonderful ways to implement strategic tax planning while you are alive or after your passing.

A trust is a separate entity with a separate tax ID number, much like your business. An estate planning attorney can help you establish a trust and even put your business proceeds into the trust. When you die, the assets bypass a process called probate. Probate is a lengthy and public process of finding your creditors and settling your affairs by a state-appointed individual after you pass away. We can't all avoid probate, but there are certain actions we can take to bypass or mitigate what assets go through the probate process. This becomes important if you have beneficiaries who need immediate access to your assets, to pay the bills. Sometimes waiting for an asset to complete the probate process is too long of a wait and will cause undue stress for your heir.

DAFs

Donor Advised Funds are a great way to pass on charitable intentions to your children. These funds are often at a mutual fund company or custodian with a minimum of $10,000 or more. The fun news is that you immediately get a tax write-off but don't have to give the money to a qualified charity immediately. Instead, the money grows over time. You then get to decide when and where to make donations out of this DAF. (You submit a "request" to the fund company for approval; chances are good that it will approve it if it's a qualified nonprofit.) DAFs can also be a great tax strategy, alternating between high- and low-income years for yourself. You also name a successor to your fund, such as your children, and pass along your intentions for the DAF in case of your demise. It's a win-win for everyone!

Family Run Businesses

Last week, my oldest daughter asked if I could hire her to do some work for my business instead of finding another person outside the family. She made a great case about how she likes using the computer to design things, using the computer to type things, and using the computer to, well, use the computer. In her 10-year-old mind, she thinks playing "business" with mom is fun, and she gets to use the computer. She doesn't understand why I would hire a stranger when I could hire her for editing, social media management, and more. I admit I felt tempted and liked seeing her sitting at my desk building something beautiful.

Many families build businesses together. Sometimes out of necessity, sometimes out of pride, and frequently out of love. There's nothing wrong with wanting to give your company to your child(ren). However, I caution anyone wanting to hand over the keys to your children to follow a checklist before doing so. Don't force the answer but be objective when looking at your child's involvement. Get someone else to answer these questions if you need an unbiased perspective.

- Does your child like your business?

- Does your child have skills to benefit the business?

- Would your child prefer the business itself or just the cash from the business?

- Will your child work as hard as you have in the business?

- Does your child have the cash to buy your business from you?

- Do you need cash from the sale of your business to fund your retirement?

- What are your child's goals, hopes, and dreams for the future? Do they align with the future of your company?

- Do you have several children who will want an interest in the business?

- Do they get along well enough to run a company together?

Family-run companies come with all sorts of baggage. Not all of it is negative; it can be a powerful organization run by family members. Passing your company to a family member is another loving way to pass on your legacy.

Whatever way you decide to pass along your legacy, I encourage you to act in the most efficient and productive way possible. Each iteration improves the world for the better. We have an obligation to the next generation to teach them our successes and failures.

A word about YOU...

Passing on a legacy is hard work. It's tiring and often thankless. You endure sleepless nights and back-breaking work. I encourage you to put the oxygen mask on yourself before worrying about your legacy and "who." Two things will prevent you from accomplishing this goal.

First, your health must always come number one. Your body is a temple, and in whatever way you move, your body is a blessing. Some of us are fortunate enough to move with grace and ease across a frozen pond. Some of us have strong legs that can kick a ball or snowboard down the highest mountains. Some of us have limitations but can still sing or draw. Use your body in such a way that you preserve your longevity. Focus on good nutrition and movement that brings you joy. If your body cannot accomplish your tasks, doing everything you need to scale and sell your business won't be easy. It's not impossible, but running a business without your health supporting your efforts is challenging. The same idea applies to the health of your mind.

Second, know that your imposter syndrome will affect your legacy for the worse. We all have doubts and secrets that keep us in the shadows sometimes. We all know our limitations and often judge ourselves harshly because of them. Let me remind you, sister, that life is short. Journal about it, shout it out, get a therapist, and do whatever it takes to address your imposter syndrome head-on.

**Your success depends on you
being the best version of yourself.**

And honey, we don't have time for you to wallow in self-doubt and pity. As I always say, "Put on your big girl pants because we have work to do." The more you second-guess yourself, the smaller your company will stay. Your imposter syndrome lessens the impact you will have on your "who" and, ultimately, your legacy. Even Mother Teresa, in the highlight of her life, when she was saving souls and caring for the sick, doubted her own abilities.[14] She drew on a greater strength and borrowed what she needed to accomplish her tasks. If that's what you must do to overcome your imposter syndrome, then do it!

There was once a local candy and gift shop owner named Margot. She was single and wildly successful. Margot had several locations in town, but the flagship store was her favorite. In this store was a giant taffy machine where the employees still made taffy daily. Tourists would come in and see the giant metal arms stretching and pulling the strings of taffy. The

---

[14] Teresa, Mother. *No Greater Love: Edited by Becky Benenate & Joseph Durepos.* New World Library, 1989.

store smelled like Christmas every day of the year and brought smiles to everyone.

Margot had a hard upbringing. Her mother died when she was young, and her father was never around. Her siblings scattered. Margot never knew the true meaning of family, so she desperately wanted to make a version of her own family. However, Margot partied. A lot. She drank heavily, traveled often, and lived as if she didn't care. She never settled down, although she had many flings in different countries. When she turned 55, a doctor diagnosed Margot with an aggressive disease that quickly spread throughout her body.

Never having her own biological family, she reflected on the family that she did have: her best friend who never left her side, her long-term employees who would bend over backwards for her, her nieces and nephews who idolized everything she did. Margot realized she had little time left to leave the true legacy she wanted. She wished she had cared for herself better and planned for the inevitable. (*This story is true, although I've changed the details to keep Margot's identity private.*)

Margot ultimately passed on a legacy the way she always dreamed of doing. She left her fortune and candy stores to her dear trusted store manager, who had been with her since the beginning. Margot cared for her nieces, nephews, and employees financially before she left. Margot's best friend helped facilitate all Margot's last wishes, which was a true gift. To this day, Margot's name brings tears of joy to many people's eyes.

What do you want your legacy to reveal about you? How will you leave the next generation better than your generation? What will your business provide for your "who's"? I believe in you with all my heart and know that what you are building is beautiful and needed today. Thank you for gifting the world with your business and brilliance. Now, go forth and do!

Made in the USA
Monee, IL
06 October 2023

44041346R00090